A JOHN CATT PUBLICATION

Zoe & Mark

T0266103

FIORELLA & MAYER'S
GENERATIVE LEARNING
IN ACTION

IN ACTION
SERIES

EDITOR
TOM
SHERRINGTON

FOREWORD BY LOGAN FIORELLA
ILLUSTRATIONS BY OLIVER CAVIGLIOLI

A
WALKTHRUs
PRODUCTION

First Published 2020

by John Catt Educational Ltd,
15 Riduna Park, Station Road,
Melton, Woodbridge IP12 1QT

Tel: +44 (0) 1394 389850
Email: enquiries@johncatt.com
Website: www.johncatt.com

Opinions expressed in this publication are those of the contributors
and are not necessarily those of the publishers or the editors. We
cannot accept responsibility for any errors or omissions.

ISBN: 978 1 913622 20 6

Set and designed by John Catt Educational Limited

TABLE OF CONTENTS

SERIES FOREWORD
TOM SHERRINGTON

The idea for the *In Action* series was developed by John Catt's *Teaching WalkThrus* team after we saw how popular our Rosenshine's Principles in Action booklets proved to be. We realised that the same approach might support teachers to access the ideas of a range of researchers, cognitive scientists and educators. A constant challenge that we wrestle with in the world of teaching and education research is the significant distance between the formulation of a set of concepts and conclusions that might be useful to teachers and the moment when a teacher uses those ideas to teach their students in a more effective manner, thereby succeeding in securing deeper or richer learning. Sometimes so much meaning is lost along that journey, through all the communication barriers that line the road, that the implementation of the idea bears no relation to the concept its originator had in mind. Sometimes it's more powerful to hear from a teacher about how they implemented an idea than it is to read about the idea from a researcher or cognitive scientist directly – because they reduce that distance; they push some of those barriers aside.

In our *In Action* series, the authors and their collaborative partners are all teachers or school leaders close to the action in classrooms in real schools. Their strategies for translating their subjects' work into practice bring fresh energy to a powerful set of original ideas in a way that we're confident will support teachers with their professional learning and, ultimately, their classroom practice. In doing so, they are also paying their respects to the original researchers and their work. In education, as in so many walks of life, we are standing on the shoulders of giants. We believe that our selection of featured researchers and papers represents some of the most important work done in the field of education in recent times.

Mark and Zoe Enser are prolific bloggers and writers, both able to communicate the essence of an idea in such a way that makes it feel simultaneously rigorous but also simple and doable. Their presentation of Fiorella and Mayer's superb work on generative learning is a perfect example.

Finally, in producing this series, we would like to acknowledge the significant influence of the researchED movement that started in 2013, run by Tom Bennett.

I was present at the first conference and, having seen the movement go from strength to strength over the intervening years, I feel that many of us, including several *In Action* authors, owe a significant debt of gratitude to researchED for providing the forum where teachers' and researchers' ideas and perspectives can be shared. We are delighted, therefore, to be contributing a share of the royalties to researchED to support them in their ongoing non-profit work.

FOREWORD
LOGAN FIORELLA

As educators, we don't just want students to recall facts. Factual knowledge is important, of course, but we want more than that. We want students to *understand* what they've learned so they can apply their knowledge to new situations. We want them to go beyond the lesson and see its implications for future learning and problem solving. In short, we want to foster *generative learning*.

Generative learning involves 'making sense' of our experience by testing it against what we already know. To illustrate, imagine you are in an airport terminal and someone frantically sprints past you with their luggage. You think to yourself, 'They must be late for their flight.' This situation makes sense because it coheres with your knowledge of airports. But notice how you didn't just observe the behaviour; you *made* sense of it – you *generated* a plausible explanation of the behaviour. Of course, sometimes things don't make sense – that is, we struggle to generate a plausible explanation of the situation ('Why is that person running through the museum?').

Although we are natural sense-makers, our desire for meaning doesn't always translate to learning abstract concepts in the classroom. Indeed, many students do not engage in generative learning spontaneously, or they struggle to do so effectively. In one study, we found most college students learning about the human respiratory system took notes by copying words and phrases (and sometimes entire sentences) directly from the lesson rather than trying to build a coherent 'mental model' of how the system works. Needless to say, these students did not develop a robust understanding of human respiration. Unfortunately, the default for many is to approach learning as a passive tape recorder rather than as an active sense-maker.

What can teachers do to foster generative learning? Over the past 40 years, cognitive scientists and educational psychologists have made substantial progress answering this question, and from this work, some important themes have emerged. In 2015, Rich Mayer and I reviewed the vast literature on learning strategies in our book *Learning as a Generative Activity*. We identified eight simple activities shown to promote student understanding across many studies:

7

summarising, mapping, drawing, self-testing, self-explaining, teaching, and enacting. Each activity supports a common set of processes reflected by what we called the select-organize-integrate model (SOI): *select* key ideas, *organize* them into a coherent structure, and *integrate* them with prior knowledge. We also used the available evidence to specify when and for whom each strategy is likely to be most effective.

It was clear from our book that research on generative learning had promising implications for improving student learning. However, until now, talk about generative learning has largely been confined to research laboratories and technical handbooks. *Generative Learning in Action* takes our work an important step further by providing teachers a concise, practical guide for how to apply principles of generative learning to real-world classroom settings. It provides concrete examples of how each generative strategy works across learning contexts, while being sensitive to potential boundary conditions. I am confident *Generative Learning in Action* will help you discover tangible ways to foster sense-making and meaningful learning in your students.

As you embark on your journey to put generative learning into action, it may be helpful to keep in mind this fundamental principle: generative learning depends on the *quality* of what students generate – the quality of their summaries, explanations, drawings, etc. It depends on generating appropriate relationships that lead to the construction of a coherent, testable, and useful model of how things work and how to solve problems in a given domain – whether it's Newton's laws, the human circulatory system, or Shakespeare.

Ultimately, learning depends on what students think about, and what students think about depends on what they already know. If students do not have sufficient background knowledge and instructional guidance to generate meaning from a lesson, the lesson simply won't make sense. This means, as teachers, we must continually be in touch with what our students know. Fortunately, generative activities not only serve as effective learning strategies but also serve as great assessment tools for gaining insight into the quality of students' knowledge. By analysing student drawings, for instance, teachers may better detect common misconceptions that can inform subsequent instruction. Furthermore, the experience of struggling while creating a drawing can send a powerful signal to students that something doesn't quite fit. In this way, generative learning is a dynamic, iterative, and communicative transaction between teachers and students.

Reading *Generative Learning in Action* is a perfect opportunity to engage in your own generative learning. How does generative learning relate to your own conception of teaching and learning? How are these strategies similar to or different from your current teaching practice? How might your students respond to generative activities? And most important, what does generative learning look like *in action*?

Logan Fiorella is assistant professor at the Department of Educational Psychology (Applied Cognition and Development) at the University of Georgia and co-author of *Learning as a Generative Activity.*

INTRODUCTION
FROM TEACHING TO LEARNING

This is an exciting time in education, especially for any teachers with an interest in educational research. The researchED movement holds conferences all over the world, with a series of books published looking at issues as diverse as SEND, curriculum and direct instruction. *Impact*, the journal of the Chartered College of Teaching, has been published for the last couple of years and is brimming with articles, often from classroom teachers, on the application of research in the classroom.

What a great deal of educational research adopted by teachers has tended to focus on is the instruction phase of the learning process. Rosenshine's 'Principles of Instruction' provides an excellent series of pointers in how a teacher can ensure that they present information in a way that increases the chance of it being learnt by the pupil. Likewise, the principles of cognitive load theory set out how instruction can be planned in a way to best manage the cognitive load of a task and so avoid overwhelming the limited working memory.

What this book does in contrast is to look at the process from the other side of the desk. Generative learning considers the learning experience from the point of view not of the teacher, but of the learner. It asks what they should do with the instruction that they have been given to ensure that they are able to truly make sense of it and learn it in a way that allows them to apply it to new situations in the future. We could see generative learning as the reverse side of Rosenshine's coin.

The book you are holding, *Generative Learning in Action*, is based on a theory of learning that suggests pupils create understanding of what is to be learnt through a process of selecting information, organising it and then integrating it into what they already know. It draws primarily on the work of Logan Fiorella and Richard E. Mayer and their 2015 book *Learning as a Generative Activity: Eight Learning Strategies that Promote Understanding*, but we also draw on the work that influenced them and on further theories of learning that we have found useful in implementing generative strategies in our classrooms.[1]

---

1. Fiorella, L. and Mayer, R. E. (2015) *Learning as a generative activity: eight learning strategies that promote understanding.* New York, NY: Cambridge University Press. (All subsequent references in parentheses will be to this text.)

Primarily this book is a teacher-eye view on what could otherwise remain an academic theory. It will explain Fiorella and Mayer's titular eight learning strategies and discuss their use in practice. We have tried to be clear on how these strategies could be deployed most effectively in a range of subjects and settings but have also, I hope, pulled no punches when it comes to discussing potential pitfalls to be avoided.

The place of generative learning in the education landscape

In order to best understand the application of generative learning in the classroom, it helps to recognise how it fits into other elements of our practice. This awareness will help us to implement the eight strategies effectively and with an awareness of potential pitfalls to avoid.

Constructivism

Generative learning falls into a broadly constructivist model of learning in which learning is viewed as something that happens in the mind of each learner and is shaped by their own experiences and the prior knowledge that they bring to the topic. For example, if I were to be presented with information about the salt plains of the Danakil Depression and the way the shallow seas evaporated leaving the mineral behind, I would link this to knowledge I already hold about plate tectonic movement in this region and the rifting that occurred there and see this new information in light of that. Someone else might already know something about the impact of salt on trade in North Africa and so will read this new information in those terms. We would both take something different from the presentation of the same material. This would suggest that learning is a highly individual thing.

As Richard Fox points out, however, this is little more than common sense, and he warns that constructivist claims about learning can be both vague and misleading:[2]

> This vague idea, itself misleading and incomplete, can be developed in a number of ways that are not always compatible with one another. Moreover, as the claims become more bold and distinctive, they risk collapsing either into implausible philosophical positions or becoming empirically too narrow, respecting some aspects and types of learning to the detriment of others.[3]

2. Fox, R. (2001) 'Constructivism examined', *Oxford Review of Education* 27 (1) pp. 23–35.
3. Ibid. p. 24

So, to take the above example, should we assume that there is no objective truth about the Danakil Depression that can be taught? That any knowledge is subjective and true only to the person holding it? These are the sort of 'bold and distinctive' yet 'implausible philosophical positions' that some radical constructivists[4] reach.

One of Fox's criticisms of constructivism in particular can highlight potential pitfalls of generative learning that we as teachers should be aware of: *learning is an active process*. This is one of the key tenets of generative learning – that pupils need to go beyond passively being around the thing to be learnt and actively engage in it. In their introduction to 'Eight Ways to Promote Generative Learning', Fiorella and Mayer cite Wittrock (1989) in saying 'the mind ... is not a passive consumer of information'; rather, 'it actively constructs its own interpretations of information and draws inferences on them'.[5] However, as Fox points out, the human mind does both. It is perfectly capable of consuming information passively and responding to it – such as the iris narrowing when exposed to bright sunlight or the way our behaviour may change as a result of some sort of sanction – without us ever being aware that this had occurred. He explains, 'Our ability to perceive, to learn, to speak and to reason are all based on the innate capacities of the evolved human nervous system.'[6]

All this really means is that we should be aware that although pupils can generate learning through the constructive and interactive methods discussed in Fiorella and Mayer's work, it would be a mistake to think they can *only* generate learning in these ways.

---

4. Glasersfeld, E. von (1993) 'Learning and adaptation in the theory of *constructivism*', *Communication and Cognition* 26 (3/4) pp. 393–402.
5. Wittrock (1989) cited in Fiorella, L. and Mayer, R. E. (2016) 'Eight ways to promote generative learning', *Educational Psychology Review* 28 (4) pp. 717–741.
6. Fox, R. (2001) p. 26

Schema theory

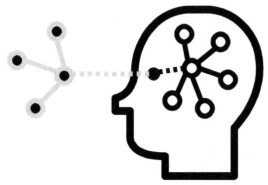

When we think about constructing meaning, we often mean constructing *schema*. This term, which relates to how the mind stores information in the long-term memory. is used in both cognitive science and psychology. Perhaps most famously, Jean Piaget looked at how cognitive function categorised and organised information in internal structures.[7] This was then developed further by Frederick Bartlett,[8] who made links to the schema and memory in psychology, which he stated involved 'an active organization of past reactions or experiences'.[9] This was later developed by R.C. Anderson, who linked ideas of schema to educational psychology, especially in regards to reading, arguing that 'every act of comprehension involves one's knowledge of the world as well'.[10] This is a statement which has significant implications for how we ensure learners have the required prior knowledge in order to access new information.

A schema (a singular collection of concepts; plural 'schemata'/'schemas') is a network of information built around connected ideas. We have a huge range of schemata which include social schemata which tell us how to behave in certain social situations (for example, how to interact with friends), events schemata (for example, in professional interactions) and personal schemata which hold certain information about ourselves, our behaviour and our abilities. Most importantly in the context of education, we hold academic schemata, where we organise and categorise information about the topics and subjects we study.

7. Piaget, J. (1926) *The language and thought of the child*. London: Kegan Paul, Trench, Trübner, & Co.
8. Bartlett, F. C. (1932) Remembering. Cambridge: Cambridge University Press.
9. An, S. (2003) 'Schema theory in reading', *Theory and Practice in Language Studies* 3 (1) pp. 130–134.
10. Ibid.

Schemata are not static stores of information and will be regularly adding information and reorganising them in order to assimilate new knowledge and develop new applications. Nor are they simply an ever-filling pail where we pour more information. Schemata are continuously involved in interactions between prior knowledge and new information which we are receiving, selecting and organising before integrating into the long-term memory (the SOI model – see below).

When we receive new information about a topic, we draw on our prior knowledge in order to make connections and create meaning. Decontextualised or seemingly random information is difficult to process, so activating prior learning, highlighting links or providing a 'big picture' within which learners can place this information will help support schema development. For example, if I were to say to you 'Danakil Depression', as I did above, but then simply walked away, it is unlikely you would remember the term. It would hold no meaning to you. Perhaps, you would mistakenly file it under 'a mental health condition'. However, you now know it is a landform feature created by tectonic movement, is found in East Africa and is involved in the production of salt. This information, 'Danakil Depression', has been given context and can now be assimilated into your schema.

It is also important to note that schemata can, and often do, contain inaccurate information and even false learning. These are the misconceptions which we see students really want to cling on to. For example, those who insist that February only has one 'r' in it or those who claim that it is hottest on the equator because it is closest to the sun These schemata need to be challenged and broken down in order to be rebuilt around the correct information. Certain misconceptions held in schemata which may have formed the basis of some of our students' earliest learning experiences are incredibly important to restructure as this may continue to impact on the further development of the correct schema, for example with issues with phonemic awareness. If some of this is not correctly understood, both reading and writing can be negatively impacted. To return to the example above, if you thought that East Africa was free from tectonic processes or had no natural resources, your schema would have to shift to accommodate contradictory information. And in this way, we generate learning.

The SOI model

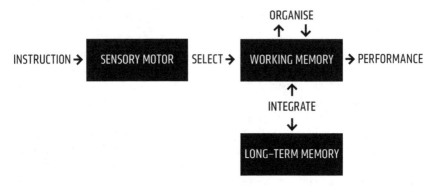

As well as being part of the constructivist tradition of learning, generative learning also falls more specifically within the cognitive constructivist tradition in that it concerns itself with models of how the mind works to help explain the learning process. One model it relies on heavily is Mayer's SOI model of memory. This model suggests that learning occurs by the mind going through three processes:

- Selection – the mind has to decide which parts of the incoming sensory information to pay attention to.

- Organisation – the mind then has to place this information into some kind of context in order to consider how to make sense of it.

- Integration – finally, the incoming information is linked to the learner's prior knowledge and is assimilated into the schema, or else the schema is altered to accommodate something that contradicts what was previously known.[11]

When information is put together in this way, the mind can generate learning. Fiorella and Mayer describe this form of learning as 'a process of making sense, in which you try to understand what is presented by actively selecting relevant pieces of information, mentally organising them, and integrating them with other knowledge you already have' (p. vii).

---

11. Mayer, R. E. (2014) 'Cognitive theory of multimedia learning' in Mayer, R. E. (ed.) *The Cambridge handbook of multimedia learning*. 2nd edn. New York, NY: Cambridge University Press, pp. 43–71.

Cognitive load theory

The SOI model uses the same kind of multi-store memory model as cognitive load theory (CLT). This model suggests that the mind is assailed with information constantly and this information is held in our sensory memory for just a fraction of a second. Our attention picks up on some of this information and this is then held in our working memory. For example, where I am now sat I can see piles of books and pieces of paper, various pens and pictures. I can hear a dog barking in the distance and the sound of a radio playing elsewhere in the house. I can still smell the slightly burnt toast from breakfast and the unlit scented candle by my desk. All of this information would hit my senses whether I was aware of it or not; only by paying deliberate attention to it have I become aware. Almost all incoming information is discarded without us knowing.

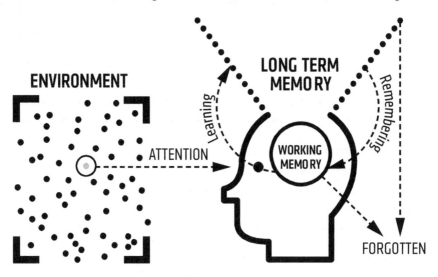

Once information is in our working memory, we can think about it. Our working memory is very limited and can only hold a few pieces of information at any one time, which it has to rehearse constantly to avoid forgetting (think about how you have to repeat a phone number to yourself as you desperately look for a pen. If something else enters your working memory whilst you are doing this, the numbers are lost). Generative learning is taking place in the working memory. It is here that new information can be thought about and processed and linked to prior knowledge.

This is because the working memory is linked to our long-term memory. This memory store is, for all intents and purposes, limitless. Our long-term memory contains our schema, our web of interconnected knowledge, about any given topic. This schema allows us to do things without troubling our limited working memory as they have become automated. Every time we draw something out of our long-term memory, the ability to recall it again becomes stronger. The goal of generative learning is to encode things strongly into our long-term memory and to make them easy to recall in the future.

Cognitive load theory suggests that any task we do places a 'load' on our working memory. If the load is too great, our working memory capacity will be overwhelmed and we won't be able to learn it. This load comes from two sources. The first is the intrinsic load, which is how complex the task itself is. The second is the extrinsic load, which is everything else in our environment or in the way the task is designed.[12] For example, there is an intrinsic load in asking pupils to work out 354 ÷ 7, but the load would be greater if we added the distracting sounds of gunfire or asked them to work it out in a novel way they hadn't encountered before.

We may wish to consider CLT when planning generative learning strategies as we want to ensure that pupil attention is being given to incoming sensory information that will help them to learn, and we want to ensure that the activity itself isn't so complex that it adds to the extrinsic load and risks overwhelming the working memory capacity.

Self-regulated learners – self efficacy and independence
One of the key aims of generative learning strategies is to develop metacognitive skills through the process, which will then motivate students through self-regulation and self-efficacy to become independent learners – the ultimate aim for many educators. Fiorella and Mayer call metacognition and motivation the 'Mighty Ms' (p. 10) and metacognitive strategies are woven throughout generative learning strategies as examined in their work.

Metacognition, in its most simple definition, is thinking about how we learn. The most successful learners are able to reflect on their learning processes, considering the strategies they have available to them to tackle different problems, selecting the most appropriate ones to apply to the task in hand, whilst developing an awareness of their strengths and gaps in their own learning. This allows them to have greater agency over their learning, making

---

12. Sweller, J. (1988) 'Cognitive load during problem solving: effects on learning', *Cognitive Science* 12 (2) pp. 257–285.

decisions not only in relation to strategies they could employ but also in terms of what they need to restudy in order to close any gaps in knowledge and understanding. Here we have students who are in control of regulating their own learning or, as B.J. Zimmerman describes them in his *Handbook of Self-Regulation and Learning Performance*,[13] self-regulated learners who 'personally activate and sustain cognitions, affects, and behaviors that are systematically oriented toward the attainment of learning goals'.[14] This is a learner who is motivated to drive their own learning forward and is therefore able to engage with learning activities in a much more independent way. They have the self-efficacy available to know that it is within their ability to solve new and complex problems as they reflect back on their past learning experiences and successes. Students who have good self-efficacy are also much more motivated in their learning, primed to work towards personal goals and use a range of effective strategies to achieve them.

Each of the generative learning strategies is designed to teach students strategies which allow them to actively engage in their own learning and reflect back on what they have, and have not, learnt and set their own goals to progress towards.

The research origins of generative learning

So, if we put together the various theories and models of learning discussed above, we can see that generative learning is based upon the idea that, for learning to take place, students must engage in a number of generative cognitive processes, after which they are able to transfer what they have learnt into solving new problems. Fiorella and Mayer use the definition of learning in their work which was discussed above in light of the SOI model of learning. This SOI model of learning also makes clear that we are a 'pattern-seeking species' who seek to 'make sense and order from the world around us'.[15] As we interact with the world around us, we are in the continuous process of collating information into our existing understanding to create new meanings and understanding.

Generative learning is also related to research into 'transferable knowledge and skills', as discussed by Pellegrino and Hilton in 2012,[16] and ways in which independent learners can be developed using various computer-based platforms.

---

13. Zimmerman, B. J. and Schunk, D. H. (2011) *Handbook of self-regulation of learning and performance*. Abingdon: Routledge.

14. Ibid, p. 1

15. Myatt, M. (2018) *The curriculum: gallimaufry to coherence*. Woodbridge: John Catt Educational, p. 23.

16. Pellegrino, J. W. and Hilton, M. L. (2012) *Education for life and work: developing transferable knowledge and skills in the 21st century*. Washington, DC: National Academies Press.

Its research origins can furthermore be found firmly rooted in the work of Piaget (1926) and Bartlett (1932), the latter of whom developed the idea of learning as 'an act of construction' in which new information is assimilated into existing schemata (p. 15). This idea that learning is based on an architecture of the mind in which memory and understanding is constructed and, perhaps even more importantly, reconstructed, is the main focus of generative learning as a theory.

Like Bartlett, Piaget's work on schemata also focuses on the idea that learning and the cognitive processes involved are more than the act of memorisation (research extended by Katone in 1940[17] and Wertheimer in 1959[18]) and that it is how we select, organise, collate and then finally integrate this information into new schemata which is important.

However it was not until the 1970s and the extensive work of Merlin C. Wittrock that the concept of generative learning was developed. Wittrock explored the relationships between existing knowledge and concluded that 'people tend to generate ... meanings that are consistent with prior knowledge', and that, with the right activities, we generate strong links between new and prior learning. This idea is a powerful one for educators and learners as they seek to find ways to embed information and knowledge. As John Hattie and Gregory Yates remind us in *Visible Learning and the Science of How We Learn*, 'New information that cannot be related to existing knowledge is quickly shed.'[19]

These ideas that underpin generative learning then led Fiorella and Mayer to a series of activities which, they argue, actively encourage students to select information from the learning materials which they can then organise and integrate into the schemata alongside their prior knowledge on the topic. This is a list of the activities which they found to be the most effective in terms of generative learning, but there are other activities which could fall within this definition:

1. Summarising

2. Mapping

3. Drawing

4. Imagining

---

17. Katona, G. (1940) *Organizing and memorizing.* New York, NY: Columbia University Press.
18. Wertheimer, M. (1959) *Productive thinking.* New York, NY: Harper & Row.
19. Hattie, J. and Yates, G. (2014) *Visible learning and the science of how we learn.* Abingdon: Routledge.

5. Self-testing

6. Self-explaining

7. Teaching

8. Enacting

Fiorella and Mayer examined research undertaken for each of these activities and determined effect size, possible applications in the classroom and boundary conditions. Our book will aim to build on their work, and the work of those they draw on, by looking at each of these activities from the perspective of a classroom teacher putting them into action.

Research base and effect size

The table below relates to the studies cited by Fiorella and Mayer and indicates the number of valid tests where key conditions were met and how many of these had a positive effect size (vs no strategy used). It is worth noting that some strategies have a much higher research base than others, and where this has been considered to be of significance, it has been explored in the coming chapters. (For a full list of all the research studies used, please refer to the original text.)

STRATEGY	POSITIVE/RESEARCH BASE	EFFECT SIZE
Summarisation	26/30	0.5
Mapping	23/25	0.62
Drawing	25/28	0.4
Imagining	16/22	0.65
Self-testing	44/47	0.62
Self-explaining	44/54	0.61
Teaching	17/19	0.77
Enacting	36/44	0.51

1 SUMMARISING

EFFECT SIZE: 0.5

DEFINITION Restate the main ideas of a lesson in one's own words.

RESEARCH Beneficial in 26 of 30 studies.

BOUNDARY CONDITIONS Best when summary skills directly taught. Less effective when lesson content contains complex spatial relations, as in physics and chemistry.

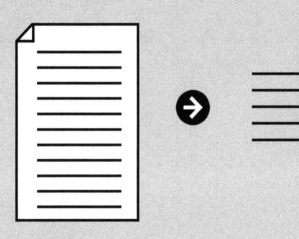

CHAPTER 1
LEARNING BY SUMMARISING

What is learning by summarising?

Before you begin to read this chapter, just take a few minutes to recap what you have learnt about generative learning so far. You can either write a short summary or summarise it verbally.

Now consider:

- What processes did you go through in order to be able to summarise?

- What information did you select?

- How did you decide what should go first in your summary?

- Did you reorganise anything?

Summary is a process which we use all the time, as we retell stories, think about earlier conversations and reflect on what we may have done yesterday. We don't go over every detail; we abbreviate, select important points and redact what we do not need in order to distil the essence of these things.

Summarising in terms of generative learning is employing these same processes, requiring students to collate and reorganise the main points from their learning at different points in the learning process. This can mean producing longer summaries at the end of a learning sequence, or interspersing summary in order to support their comprehension. Summaries can be verbal or textual, and there are benefits and restrictions with both.

This is most effective where the learning isn't reliant on material which is spatially complex; for example, diagrams and tables in a science textbook, where ideas have already been condensed or synthesised.

Why use learning by summarising?

When asking students to summarise, we are asking them to engage again with the 'select', 'organise' and 'integrate' cognitive processes of generative learning.

Summarising, according to Wittrock,[20] is an effective generative approach as it 'forces students to engage with the generative strategies' (p. 24). This activity means they have to extract the key information, make links and associations within the new material and then make associations with material which is already stored in their existing schemata. This, he concludes, will lead to deeper learning.

Moreover, using single-sentence summaries, where students write or verbalise a summary after each paragraph, significantly supports the comprehension of students with 'lower' reading abilities but is also important for those with a 'higher' reading ability (p. 24). This could indicate that the process of summarising short sections of learning can support the students' ability to select key information.

Summarisation has been shown to boost learning and retention as it requires students to attend to both the higher meaning of the material and the gist of it. Studies by Bretzing and Kulhavy (1979)[21] and Craik and Lockhart (1972) both indicated that summarisation yielded greater benefits in terms of comprehension due to the requirement to manipulate material in order to form cohesive summaries.

Furthermore, Peper and Meyer examined the relationship between note-taking, summary and learning outcomes. They found that students who take notes but couple this with summary at the end of their notes performed 10–15% better than their peers who just took notes in problem-solving assessment and 13–17% better in recall than those who did not summarise their learning.[22]

How to use summarisation in the classroom

Summary has long been a staple in the English classroom. Indeed it is a key component of one of the assessment objectives in the English Language GCSE, where students need to show they can select and synthesise information from texts, often appearing in the form of a summary question.

In English, I have frequently asked students to summarise key points from a text we are reading, limiting them to no more than 30 words – sometimes reducing that to no more than 10 – to ensure that they have retained the salient points.

20. Wittrock, M. C. (1974) 'Learning as a generative process', *Educational Psychologist* 11 (2) pp. 87–95; Wittrock, M. C. (1989) 'Generative processes of comprehension', *Educational Psychologist* 24 (4) pp. 345–376.
21. Dunlosky, J. et al. (2013) 'Improving students' learning with effective learning techniques: promising directions from cognitive and educational psychology', *Psychological Science in the Public Interest* 14 (1) pp. 4–58, p. 11.
22. Busch, B. and Watson, E. (2019) *The science of learning: 77 studies that every teacher needs to know.* Abingdon: Routledge, p. 69.

These are then shared and discussed in order to explore which elements have been chosen, which may have been omitted and if this is a clear representation of the section. This is a way in which I encourage the development of metacognitive strategies as students reflect on their learning and how they have presented it in their summary form. I also ensure that some of their summary work is closed book, ensuring that they pay much greater attention to the original learning materials and give them opportunities to make connections between different information in their summaries, for example summarising the ideas about gender in two poems.

I have often used shorter, single-sentence (or even single-word) summaries to support comprehension of complex or longer texts, encouraging students to write their own paragraph summaries in the margin, identifying or creating topic sentences to support them. This allows me to quickly check that students have an understanding of the gist of the text and also ensures that false learning is not becoming embedded. Again, this enables students to reflect on their own learning, exploring the text in small steps and demonstrating how their overall understanding of the text has developed.

Using Cornell notes is another effective method which can combine different generative learning strategies discussed in this book: summary, drawing, mapping and self-testing. It can be an effective strategy across all subjects and works for lectures, videos and use of textbook resources.

In this method, students are given a divided page where they make notes during a lecture or whilst studying, add questions or identify key points in the margin and write a textual summary at the bottom.

As students take notes in the main section, they can include diagrams, maps and drawings, as well as keywords and phrases that are located at the relevant part of their notes. They select and organise the information, supporting their summary, in which they continue these processes and incorporate information from their prior learning, drawing on prior knowledge and strengthening and building on existing schemata. (There is more detail regarding using Cornell notes in the case study for this section.)

Learning by summarising across the curriculum

- In **history**, when reading a longer text, the learner could summarise either line by line or each paragraph.

- In **science**, after watching a video clip explaining a principle, the learner could select the key information and organise it into a summary. This could be done either verbally or in writing.

- In **PE**, after watching a demonstration from the teacher, the learner could be asked to summarise to the rest of the class the key points to remember.

Case study of learning by summarising

Adam Riches is an assistant principal, head of English and author of *Teach Smarter*. In this case study, he explains how he has taught his pupils to use a strategy for summarising that he himself found useful as a student.

Cornell note-taking isn't something that is new to me. I was first introduced to it at university by my American lecturer when we were discussing computational linguistics. At the time, I was struggling to pick out the key information during lectures about topics, and he showed me how I could condense my notes into a much more succinct and formulated revision tool. Of course, at the time, I didn't consider the learning benefit from a teaching perspective, and because of this it was some time before I revisited the method in an academic context.

Something that is apparent is that a lot of things in education are assumed, especially when you pick up a class later in their school life. One of the common assumptions is that students know how to take notes…mainly because they automatically (most of them) write when they are in lessons. Often, they know how to follow instructions and engage from the board, but, when you drill down, they have no idea how to take notes because they have never been taught.

It follows that when students then revise independently, without a teacher to give instructions and a board to follow on, they simply resort to default: they write down everything – much like me at university. There might be some titles and highlighting, but for the most part, the notes will be very general. This makes the information encoded within those words harder to access and it also means that the process in which they were recorded was most likely very passive.

To combat this shortcoming, I resorted to teaching Cornell note-taking early in year 10. By introducing students to an alternative way to take notes, which significantly surpasses rote note-taking, I was able to not only foster more confidence in the analysis of texts and decoding of teaching but also teach self-efficacy. This allowed much more efficient and valuable independent study and, best of all, much richer outcomes from the reams of information available for students online.

Starting with the most basic approach, I adopt the idea of breaking the page up to have a clear title, one column for key points/key ideas being discussed and one column for notes. At the bottom of the page, a summary box finishes off the sheet. Nothing flash and of course, although taking the Cornell format, I don't often encourage pages and pages of notes – the students aren't in lectures after all.

As an introduction, I actually populate the key point/key idea box for the students as a way of modelling the approach and scaffolding their adoption of the technique. As the scaffolding is gradually withdrawn, they fill in this box by themselves. The right-hand box could (and should) be filled with any note-taking that the students wish – words, pictures, diagrams, mind maps – it's totally up to them; but for me, I always say no sentences. This allows the students the opportunity to break free of the confines of long-winded encoding.

The summary box is the most important for me and I stress the importance of completing this in the right way. This is where understanding is checked and misconceptions can be quickly picked up by the teacher. Flicking through 30 summary boxes or circulating and checking when they are being completed can significantly reduce your marking workload and quickly highlight any misunderstandings that have emerged. Moreover, a well-written summary serves as an excellent revision tool for an idea or topic, with a fraction of the cognitive load.

Can an American university approach really be effective for students sitting their GCSEs? Yes. Not only do students buy into their learning differently, but teaching becomes significantly more efficient. More efficiency means more time; more time means more learning.

Cornell notes are great for any resource. As I've mentioned, the students are rarely lectured (although at times this approach is adopted by many and can be very effective) because secondary education is more fluid. Cornell note-taking is exceptionally good for engagement in video-based resources, when students use audio resources and when they engage with texts. The method adds clarity and logic to unseen and unheard stimuli and this makes the recording of said content much more effective than if the students had just gone at it in the traditional way.

It works. It is quick and simple to teach. It will make learning easier for your students.

Potential limitations of summarising

When using summary as a learning strategy, the highest effect is achieved when time is devoted to its direct teaching, including how to select key points, remove irrelevant material, select and generate topic sentences. Therefore, without specific instruction, students, especially those who may have limited ability to construct written or verbal summaries due to their age or verbal or written literacy, may struggle to create a successful summary of their learning. Students failing to omit irrelevant information or copying points verbatim will not be engaging with the valuable selecting and organising cognitive processes which will lead to integration and encoding into the long-term memory. Removing study notes or original learning materials can both avoid this opportunity and employ aspects of retrieval (discussed in chapter 5, 'Self-testing') which can also be seen as an effective learning strategy in itself.

The time required to invest in this strategy could therefore outweigh the potential benefits. In one study, teachers were given 90-minute training on teaching summary. This was followed by five 50-minute sessions of explicit teaching of how to produce an effective summary, in which the process was modelled and time was devoted to practising application, whilst students were coached and guided in their practice. Although students in receipt of this teaching outperformed those without this input, the level of investment required may make this approach impractical in some contexts.[23] The time cost here leads Dunlosky et al. to rate summarisation as low utility in comparison to other learning strategies.[24]

Using longer summaries infrequently can have a greater impact than frequent summary as students may expend more effort when the summaries follow a longer sequence in the learning process. Simply asking students to create summaries of their learning at numerous points could limit the impact of the learning strategy as students no longer are motivated to 'think hard' about the original learning materials.

23. Dunlosky, J. (2013) 'Strengthening the student toolbox', *American Educator 37* (3) pp. 12–21. Retrieved from www.bit.ly/2YpLDeC, p. 9.
24. Dunlosky, J. et al. (2013), p. 15.

Try it out

Use the space here to summarise your main learning points from this chapter. Think carefully about the key points you want to include (select), the order you wish to present them in (organise) and how they link to the idea of Generative Learning as a whole (integrate).

Further reading

Dunlosky, J. (2013) 'Strengthening the student toolbox', *American Educator* 37 (3) pp. 12–21. Retrieved from www.bit.ly/2YpLDeC

Allison, S. (2018) 'Supporting retrieval practice with Cornell note taking', *Class Teaching* [Blog], 24 September. Retrieved from www.bit.ly/322Rt5p

Needham, T. (2020) 'Insights from learning as a generative activity part 3: learning by summarising', *Tom Needham* [Blog], 8 June. Retrieved from www. bit.ly/3kOOCFX

DEFINITION Convert a text lesson into a spatial arrangement of connected key words.

RESEARCH Beneficial in 23 of 25 studies.

BOUNDARY CONDITIONS Best for novices – low knowledge base or young in age.

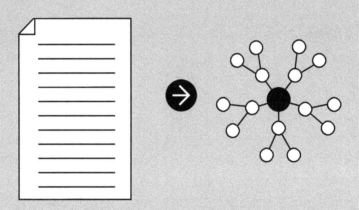

CHAPTER 2
LEARNING BY MAPPING

What is learning by mapping?

Mapping as a generative activity refers to a group of different techniques in which the learner represents text, whether written or spoken, as a spatial organisation of words with lines connecting them to show relationships. These different techniques are sometimes referred to under the blanket term 'mind maps', but thinking about the different ways they can be deployed helps us to appreciate their power in the classroom:

- A **concept map** is a network in which words represent key concepts and lines connect them to show how the words are linked. These lines are often annotated with a description of the link.

- A **knowledge map** is a more specialised form of concept map in which the links are confined to predetermined types (e.g. 'this leads to...', 'this is part of...', 'this is a characteristic of...').

- **Graphic organisers** are more specialised still and include a structure which is used to categorise information more tightly. This might include:

  - Matrix for compare and contrast

  - Flowchart for cause and effect

  - Hierarchy for classification

Why use learning by mapping?

Concept mapping can provide a number of important roles for learners. One of these is to help pupils organise what might seem like disparate information into a more logical form. John Hattie explains that 'the mind does not relate well to unstructured data ... We need to find the organisation, structure, and meaning in whatever we learn.'[25] The way we find this organisation, structure and meaning is through the construction of schemata about a topic. For example, when we see a small terrier, we recognise it as a type of dog, which we know is a mammal and therefore an animal. Each of these things might tell us

---

25. Hattie, J. (2014) *Visible learning and the science of how we learn.* Abingdon: Routledge, p. 115.

something about how to respond to this creature based on our prior knowledge and feelings about each of these categories. What mapping therefore allows us to do is create a visual representation of our emerging schema about a topic.

The creation of concept maps forces the learner to select information that they feel is relevant, which involves an active engagement with the information they have, prompting them to *think hard* and therefore to remember it. As well as thinking hard about the selection of the information, they also have to think hard about where to place it in relation to other information on their map. They need to consider how one piece of information on their map links to another or where to place it in a hierarchy. This reflects the way schemata are often organised with information categorised into a hierarchy such as 'Terrier → Dog → Canine → Mammal → Animal'.

Concept mapping also allows pupils to combine new information which is to be learnt with what they already know, their prior knowledge. This creates a hook for the new information and makes its place in a schema explicit as well as providing an opportunity to retrieve that which was learnt before, taking advantage of the testing effect (See chapter 5). For example, a learner may be creating a concept map showing the various causes for the spread of cholera in Victorian England but would need to use their prior knowledge of this period to show how these causes are connected (such as an annotated link between rapid urbanisation and a lack of effective sanitation).

How to use mapping in the classroom

Mapping as a generative activity can be used in a number of ways in the classroom. At its most simple, learners can be asked to read a text about a topic they are studying and transform it into a concept map. For example, in geography, they might read a description of Typhoon Haiyan and then produce a concept map showing its causes, effects and responses. They might decide to categorise the effects further into economic, social and environmental and they might divide the responses into immediate and long term. They may need some guidance in deciding how to categorise this information, as every discipline will have its own way of organising knowledge.

As they complete their concept map, they could then draw lines between different categories of information to show the links. For the Typhoon Haiyan concept map, they might consider a link between the economic impacts of the coast road flooding with the environmental impact of the removal of mangrove forest, or link the coast road flooding to the hampering of the response. These lines are then annotated to explain what the link is. In a knowledge map, the lines already correspond to a particular function, such as causality. In history, a knowledge map might be constructed to show the flow of events that led to the outbreak of a conflict.

One potential drawback of using mapping is that the learner may have to focus too much on the strategy of organising information and not enough on the information being learnt. Another way of using this technique, therefore, is to give a prefilled concept map or graphic organiser that the learner has to populate with relevant information. They are still engaged in generating learning through selection and, to an extent, integration, but the organisation aspect has been scaffolded. An example of this might occur in a science lesson where a graphic organiser is being used to contrast the properties of two different elements. In this case, the learner could be given at least some of the categories for comparison.

A third approach to mapping is to take further advantage of the testing effect by leaving a gap between learners encountering new information and them completing a map. Without a gap, there is a risk that pupils will transfer information from the text to their map without having to engage in much thought. This would be especially true if you were using a prefilled map as discussed above. A short gap of time can make the use of mapping a more effective strategy for learning as the learner has to think hard to select information from their memory.[26]

However mapping is used, the key principles remain the same. Pupils are asked to select information and organise it into a logical structure that builds on their prior knowledge which allows them to integrate it into their existing schema.

Learning by mapping across the curriculum

- In **MFL**, the learner might be asked to map the various ways common prefixes and suffixes are used.

- In **design technology**, the learner might turn their design proposal into a concept map and use the same headings for future plans.

- In **religious education**, the learner might use a graphic organiser to contrast the position of different faiths on a range of issues.

26. Blunt, J. R. and Karpicke, J. D. (2014) 'Learning with retrieval-based concept mapping', *Journal of Educational Psychology* 106 (3) pp. 849–858.

37

Case study of learning by mapping

Christian Moore Anderson is a biology teacher at Oak House School in Barcelona. He blogs at www.bit.ly/2EfJZUk. In this case study, he explains the importance of the teacher modelling the effective use of mapping before asking pupils to use them as generative learning strategies.

I wanted to improve the mechanistic reasoning of my students, but biology has so many complex interactions that it can be hard for students to see the wood for the trees. I decided to make a modified concept map to help reduce cognitive load.

I invented a biology-specific concept map that separates the map into three sections: the organismal, the cellular, and the molecular. This helps students as the information is already organised. I kept the maps simple, without too many entities (maybe six or seven), because the students will also have to consider the connections in the process, and its effects.

I very quickly discovered that while the maps could be made spontaneously on the board, to get the best results and cause the least confusion, it was most effective if I planned my maps for each lesson in advance. This allowed the maps to explicitly present the information in the way I wanted the students to perceive it.

When I began to use them for the first time, some students felt overwhelmed by the number of entities and arrows. When students felt lost, it helped to remind them to begin at one point and move step by step around the map until they could consider it all together.

I used different maps every lesson, adding some things, removing others, but keeping some things stable so that students could always relate back to previous classes.

The students started to get accustomed to working with them and as a useful way of visualising connections. I also used them as retrieval practice by showing them a map they had already seen but with the connections missing. By the end of the topic, I started to see real benefits in the students' writing, which now contained much more connected information.

When students gained confidence on a topic, I could ask them to produce a map for themselves to elaborate on their own knowledge. I found it was useful to limit the students to a small number of entities, however, as some students will have the propensity to dispense everything they know with little reflection.

Potential limitations of learning by mapping

As with many of the eight strategies for generative learning, there is a recommendation that children are trained in how to use the strategy effectively. This time can amount to several hours of additional time that would need to be found from the curriculum. An added complication is that there are several ways to use mapping and these may be done differently in various subjects.

Prefilled concept maps can be used so that the learner needs to spend less time considering how to structure the map, but it should be remembered that this is then reducing the use of the 'organise' component of the underpinning SOI model. There is a risk they will simply select information to transfer but not consider its role in their wider mental model.

Try it out

Organise the information from this strategy into a concept map. Take some time to first consider which information you wish to select, then how you might organise it, and then finally whether you can integrate it with prior knowledge you hold.

Further reading

Kinchin, I. M. (2016) *Visualising powerful knowledge to develop the expert student.* Rotterdam: Sense Publishing.

Weinstein, Y. and Sumeracki, M. (2019) 'Tips for students' in *Understanding how we learn.* Abingdon: Routledge.

3 DRAWING

DEFINITION Create a drawing to illustrate content of a lesson.

RESEARCH Beneficial in 26 of 28 studies.

BOUNDARY CONDITIONS Best when drawing skills directly taught, and lessening cognitive load by providing partially drawn illustrations.

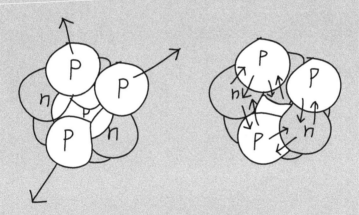

CHAPTER 3
LEARNING BY DRAWING

What is learning by drawing?

If someone was giving you complex instructions for a procedure you had to carry out, how would you make sure you learnt the steps of the process? You might decide to draw a series of images. In doing so, you would be generating learning by drawing.

This strategy refers to activities in which the learner is asked to draw an image to represent the information they wish to learn. This might involve drawing diagrams of complex processes, such as fractional distillation, or pictures to represent structure, such as the cells of a plant. Mayer suggests that drawing might be:

- Decorative, where the image serves no further purpose than to brighten up the page

- Representational, where the image simply shows an element of the lesson, such as a picture of a motte and bailey to illustrate some notes on forms of Medieval defence

- Organisational, where the drawing is combined with mapping (see chapter 2) to show the relationships between parts of a system, such as an illustration of the role different characters play in the plot of a novel

- Explanative, where the drawings show how an action in one part of a system may lead to changes elsewhere, such as a diagram of a food web that shows the impact of removing an apex predator[27]

Not all these types of drawing are generative activities. Those done to be decorative or representational rarely rely on the same kind of selection, organisation and integration that this model of learning calls on.

---

27. Mayer, R. E. (1993) 'Illustrations that instruct' in Glaser, R. (ed.) *Advances in Instructional Psychology, vol. 4.* Hillsdale, NJ: Lawrence Erlbaum Associates, pp. 253–284.

Why use learning by drawing?

Fiorella and Mayer provide extensive evidence that interventions where pupils are asked to turn text into some form of drawing lead to greater learning than that achieved by pupils in a control group who are not asked to do this (pp. 68–74). Many of these studies share similarities with the summarising and mapping strategies discussed in the previous two chapters in which learners are asked to read a text and then draw a diagram to show the processes they have read about as a summary or put the information into a graphic organiser, a form of mapping.

As with all these strategies, the same three cognitive processes underpin learning by drawing: selection, organisation and integration.

- When pupils are asked to turn a description of a process, plot or system into a drawing, they first have to think about **selecting** the relevant information from what they have read.

- Having selected the information, they then need to think hard again about its **organisation** in order to represent it on the page and consider where the information belongs in relation to anything else they need to draw.

- In the final step of **integration**, they consider the relationships between the different components of the information to reflect on how one element may affect another and how to show its links to their prior knowledge that will exist outside of the new learning material.

One benefit of learning by drawing over some other strategies, such as summarising and mapping, is that it is far less likely that the learner will be able to simply transfer information from place to place without engaging with it. The original information is in a textual or verbal form and will need to be translated into a visual form. To do this, you can't avoid engagement. This movement from a textual and verbal medium to a visual one also takes advantage of dual coding.

Dual coding theory suggests that people can process information on two different channels: an auditory channel (that includes both speech and text, which is processed by the brain as auditory information) and a visual channel.[28] By combining text and relevant images, we can avoid overloading any one channel and have two sources of information to learn from. Drawing as a generative activity usually involves drawing annotated diagrams in which the text is integrated into the image, making the material easier to learn.[29]

28. Pavio, A. (1986) *Mental representations*. New York, NY: Oxford University Press.
29. Mayer, R. E and Anderson, R. B. (1991) 'Animations need narrations: an experimental test of a dual-coding hypothesis', *Journal of Educational Psychology* 83 (4) pp. 484–490.

How to use learning by drawing in the classroom

This is not an overly complex strategy to apply to the classroom. The learner is given a textual or verbal description of a process and they are asked to turn it into a diagram; for example, a description of the process of tectonic plate movement at a divergent boundary. The reason this is generative is that they do not simply have to draw a picture; they must also consider the way different parts of the process interact – in this case, how mantle plumes might lead to ridge push with subduction as the cooling crust is pulled under the continental plate.

This need for the drawing to be generative is likely to be where this strategy is misapplied. For example, reading a description of the island in *Lord of the Flies* and attempting to draw a map is unlikely to generate a deeper understanding of the text (although it may help pupils to better learn the details of the place if that was felt to be important). However, plotting Ralph's or Jack's movements around the island and showing how the writer's use of the place is instrumental to the plot could be generative. There is now a spatial organisation of material that looks for patterns and links.

One consideration for the classroom is where the learner's attention is directed during this activity. If 'memory is the residue of thought', then we need to ensure they are thinking about the information at hand rather than the process of drawing it.[30] It is too easy to be distracted by the ephemera of the process, such as the colouring pencils used or the level of accuracy in the representation. In addition, the act of drawing places an extraneous load on the learning process if the learner is having to focus on the 'tedious mechanics of drawing'.[31] For this reason, it may be advantageous to use drawings where the outline is already provided so that the learner can focus on selecting and organising the relevant information rather than on their skill at drawing.

As with any learning strategy, it is also possible that what a learner produces will simply be incorrect. It is useful for them to see a finished and well-produced version after the task so that they can make any corrections and additions that they may have missed and consider how they could improve or refine their technique in the future.

Learning by drawing across the curriculum

- In **science**, the learner might be asked to turn a written description of processes, such as fractional distillation, into a diagram.

---

30. Willingham, D. T. (2009) *Why don't students like school? A cognitive scientist answers questions about how the mind works and what it means for the classroom.* San Francisco, CA: Jossey-Bass.
31. Fiorella, L. and Mayer, R. E. (2016) p. 724.

- In **English**, the learner might be asked to draw visual representations of the imagery used by a writer. This could be especially powerful when exploring patterns in language.

- In **art**, drawing could show the steps taken in a technique to be used.

Case study of learning by drawing

Ben Newmark – history teacher and author of *Why Teach?*, a frank appraisal of teaching's absurdities and a guide to navigating them – explains how a teacher can model the use of drawings to aid effective explanation.

Some things are much easier to understand from a picture than from text, so I often draw visual analogies and metaphors when teaching history.

An example of this might be dealing with the question as to whether Gustav Stresemann really solved German's problems between 1923 and 1929 or only appeared to do so.

Teaching this without using a picture is quite possible. It might involve using a table with two columns, one labelled 'Solved German's problems' and the other labelled 'Only appeared to solve Germany's problems'. Guided by their teacher, pupils could then populate the columns with supporting evidence for each interpretation.

There is nothing inherently wrong with this. It's fine. But I'm not convinced this really helps pupils conceptualise the historical debate around Stresemann properly.

Instead of a table, I sketch, either on the board or on paper under a visualiser, a stick figure hanging wallpaper on a cracked wall that looks as if it could fall down any minute. I label the stick figure 'Stresemann', the wallpaper 'his solutions' and the wall 'Germany in 1923'. Then I label the diagram using the same evidence that would have gone in the table, including Germany's structural problems and what Stresemann did to try to resolve them. This opens up a discussion firstly on the visual metaphor itself (What is the stick figure doing? What's he trying to hide?) and then on what the metaphor represents (What were Germany's problems? Did Stresemann really fix them or just 'cover up the cracks'?).

This rough picture then gets used a lot – it becomes a mnemonic and the basis of retrieval practice. I use it so often that pupils groan when they see me sketching it up again. And there's another benefit too: although pupils might not realise it, they're also learning exactly how a political cartoon works – always useful to know.

Potential limitations of learning by drawing

The biggest limitation of drawing is likely to be the frustration from those who feel they can't draw accurately. It can be difficult to convince them that accurate visual representation isn't the goal and that the drawing is part of the learning process, regardless of how it ends up looking. It could also be the case that a great deal of time is taken up in the action of drawing rather than in thinking about the information to be learnt and the understanding that is to be gleaned from the process.

Try it out

Think about the SOI model which has been referred to throughout this text. How would you draw an image to represent this process in the box below?

Further reading

Caviglioli, O. (2019) *Dual coding with teachers*. Woodbridge: John Catt Educational.

Mayer, R. E. (2014) *The Cambridge handbook of multimedia learning*. Cambridge, MA: Cambridge University Press.

DEFINITION Form internal images to illustrate the content of a lesson.

RESEARCH Beneficial in 16 of 22 studies.

BOUNDARY CONDITIONS Best when students have experience in the content and it is well designed.

CHAPTER 4
LEARNING BY IMAGINING

What is learning by imagining?

Close your eyes. Imagine the term 'generative learning'. What image comes to mind? Do you have a picture of something 'generating', a plant or something coming to life or growing? What images connect to this central idea? Is it being circled by things such as maps from the mapping chapter or something which represents drawing from the previous section?

This is using imagining as a generative learning strategy. The strategy asks learners to create mental images of their learning, providing prompts and ideas as necessary to support the process. Students are required to transfer verbal or textual information and create images of key elements of their learning.

Students can be asked to create:

- static image
- steps in a process
- animated sequences

Research on the effect of imagining has been conducted focusing on the recall of academic topics, for example the respiratory system; but research has also been conducted exploring the impact of mental imagining and its impact on reading comprehension, with promising results (p. 87).

As with all of the generative learning strategies, students are required to follow the three processes of generative learning, selecting the most relevant areas of their learning, organising the information into a mental image and integrating this alongside prior knowledge held within their schemata in order to create a new mental picture.

Another aspect of this approach might include asking students to create their mental image of what the respiratory system might look like on the page of a textbook and then sharing an illustration to draw comparisons and discuss how and why the information has been selected and organised in this particular way.

Why use learning by imagining?

In employing this strategy, we are again asking students to engage in the specific cognitive processes of selecting, organising and integrating. We are asking them to form connections between verbal or textual information and visual representations. Just as with mapping and drawing, we are providing students the direct opportunity to create these links, which will support the development of a schema around the learning. The links to prior learning in this process is significant here.

It is important to ensure that students do have some prior knowledge of the topic in order for this to be most successful, with the research showing a higher effect size in college students who already had schemata developed around the subject,[32] as opposed to those with development needs.[33] However, some of the research, especially in relation to comprehension, also showed good effect sizes with younger children.

This indicates the potential of the strategy in supporting the formation of schemata, with learners once again focusing on creating connections and building on their previous experiences. As Christine Counsell says, when discussing ideas relating to core and hinterland, students will be able to memorise key facts about medieval life but they 'won't understand let alone sustain precise, flexible & useful recall of those takeaways without images, landscapes, stories, varied details that give you a sense of medieval peasantness: you need to see, you need colour for mental models to form'.[34]

Imagining is one way we can support students to achieve those mental models.

Unlike concept mapping or drawing strategies, imagining has the potential to reduce extraneous cognitive load at key moments in the learning. Technical skills, especially in relation to drawing, could serve as a distraction to the main focus; and where there are very specific technical requirements, this could place increased demands on the working memory. However, imagining itself can place a load on the working memory as the image is stored here whilst being developed.

The research indicates that imagining can have specific relevance to comprehension in reading, with visualisation a frequently used strategy in the

---

32. Giesen, C. and Peeck, J. (1984) 'Effects of imagery instruction on reading and retaining literary text', *Journal of Mental Imagery* 8 (2) pp. 79–90.
33. Bender, B. G. and Levin, J. R. (1978) 'Pictures, imagery, and retarded children's prose learning', *Journal of Educational Psychology* 70 (4) pp. 583–588.
34. Counsell, C. (2020) [Twitter post]. Retrieved from www.bit.ly/326C8AJ

teaching of reading. In research conducted by Pressley in 1976, it was found that learners who were given instruction to picture elements of a 950-word story in their head significantly outperformed the control group in a subsequent comprehension test.[35]

The quality of the materials used for the initial part of the learning sequence is also important, so poor quality verbal, textual or tabulate information will lead to a lower effect from imagining.

How to use imagining in the classroom

Just as with other strategies of generative learning, it is important to give explicit instruction to students to achieve the highest effect. Creating mental images of sentences and single aspects of learning will help to build this capacity in many students. Supporting students in deciding which elements to select and which ways to organise the information by modelling metacognitive processes as part of the explicit training could also be key.

Once students are confident in knowing how to complete this process, it can be integrated into many different classroom settings. In English, this could be achieved by asking students to imagine characters or settings, selecting key elements from the text and drawing on other information they have learnt about the type of character or setting. For example, in studying the opening of *A Christmas Carol*, students would draw on their prior understanding of the setting of London, both now and in the 1800s, should this have been part of their prior learning. They may well then furnish their original image with details from the text in order to form a more detailed image around this. When considering the character of Scrooge, students may already have knowledge of the character and Victorian gentlemen in general, but can adapt this by drawing on textual details. Once they have been able to create an image to locate both character and place, they will include these within their schemata, thereby supporting their comprehension as they continue to read. In a 1993 study by Gambrell and Jawitz , cited by Fiorella and Mayer, the authors asked a group of fourth graders to read a 925-word story while making as many pictures as they could in their heads about the things they read (the imagining group). The study found that the students instructed to use imagining 'greatly outperformed the control group on a free recall test and a cued recall test' (p. 86).

After a mental model has been formed from a text, comparisons can be made to other pictorial versions – certainly easy with a much-depicted character such

---

35. Pressley, G. M. (1976) 'Mental imagery helps eight-year-olds remember what they read', *Journal of Educational Psychology* 68 (3) pp. 355–359.

as Scrooge – and discussion around comparison can be further used to explore the contents of the original text.

In a geography classroom, this strategy could be used for predictive tasks. For example, drawing on their knowledge on North Africa and climate change, two distinct topics. Students could be asked to imagine an image of the impact climate change could have on North Africa. Here we see them again selecting key information from two schemata, organising the information into a new pattern or structure and integrating this into their long-term memory. Again comparisons can be made, using alternative images.

Learning by imagining across the curriculum

- In **PE**, the learner might visualise the movements they will be carrying out in a series of stages to contrast against a model.

- In **history**, the learner could imagine the scene being described by the teacher in order to strengthen their memory of the information presented.

- In **maths**, when confronted with a problem-solving scenario, the learner may wish to imagine the scene playing out so as to consider potential mathematical solutions.

Case study of learning by imagining

In this case study, Tim Taylor – author of *A Beginner's Guide to Mantle of the Expert*, freelance teacher and trainer – explains how imagination has shaped his view of teaching as well as its practice.

Imagination is the Cinderella subject of education research. As Kieran Egan observed as long ago as 1986, 'research has largely neglected imagination, because imagination is, after all, difficult stuff to get any clear hold on'.[36]

And this is the problem. We all have imagination (although some deny their portion) and we all know how it appears in our minds, yet it is largely ignored in research and widely underused in classrooms, except when children are asked to 'write a story'.

However, some have argued (notably Egan, but also Dorothy Heathcote and others) that imagination is a powerful medium for learning and something

---

36. Egan, K. (1986) *Teaching as story telling*. London, ON: The Althouse Press.

we human beings (and maybe especially children) do without training and without considerable effort, if engaged.

I've been fascinated by the potential of using imagination since I first became a teacher and watched the children in my class busy making meaning in groups and alone while inhabiting 'imaginary worlds' of their own creation. 'What if,' I asked myself, 'that facility (which was obviously deeply engaging for the children) could be organised and planned for as a medium for curriculum teaching? That would be a powerful thing.'

It was at this point in my career that I started searching for others who had written on the subject and came across Egan and, more significantly, Dorothy Heathcote.

Heathcote, who was still writing and teaching at this time in the mid 1990s, had spent a career exploring the use of drama as a learning medium and was in the process of developing an approach that had come out of her work called 'mantle of the expert'.

Drama in the classroom, she realised, was closely aligned to play and play, she argued, is the manifestation of imagination. Therefore, her approach was to create (as a teacher) imaginary scenarios which the children could step in and out of and which would generate a context for curriculum study.

Inside the context, the children would take on the 'mantle' (that is, the responsibility) of an expert team with a mission that involved them in various activities. It was these activities, designed by the teacher, that would harness the children's imagination while developing their knowledge and understanding of the curriculum.

I've spent the last 25 years exploring Heathcote's approach and I have seen how it can transform classrooms and do that thing that I saw happening in the early years of my career, but not in a haphazard, 'leave them to get on with it and don't interfere' kind of way, but by using an organised, planned, and systematic approach that is now well understood, if still under researched.

Potential limitations of imagining as a generative strategy

This strategy works best when students have some prior knowledge of a topic and the research indicates that some students with developmental delay, or low prior attainment, may not be able to sustain mental images, especially as the image itself is held and developed in the working memory, and this can actually impair their ability to use imagining to aid their comprehension.[37,38]

Imagining can place extra load on working memory, as the mental images need to be held here as well as being used to select, organise and draw information from the long-term memory. Therefore, for tasks which may already be placing strain on working memory, this strategy may be less successful. One way to combat this may well be through creating mental images at strategic points in the learning process, when information is being introduced in small steps as recommended in explicit instruction research, for example Rosenshine's 'Principles of Instruction'.[39] Students also need to have good motivation for this strategy to be the most successful as there is no concrete outcome. They may simply not complete the task.

37. Leahy, W. and Sweller, J. (2004) 'Cognitive load and the imagination effect', *Applied Cognitive Psychology* 18 (7) pp. 857–875.
38. Leahy, W. and Sweller, J. (2005) 'Interactions among the imagination, expertise reversal, and element interactivity effects', *Journal of Experimental Psychology: Applied* 11 (4) pp. 266–276.
39. Rosenshine, B. (2012) 'Principles of instruction: research-based strategies that all teachers should know', *American Educator* 36 (1) pp. 12–19, 39. Retrieved from www.bit.ly/2Kwl7qg

Try it out

In summary, imagining requires students to select components to include in their image, organise these components into a spatial layout and integrate the information by translating it from one mode to another, for example from words into pictures.

Either close your eyes and imagine what this process of selecting and organising might look like for your subject or visualise it in the box below.

Further reading

Egan, K. (1986) *Teaching as story telling.* London, ON: The Althouse Press.

Enser, M. (2019) 'Tell it like a story if you want them to learn', *Tes [Online], 17 February.* Retrieved from www.bit.ly/318eV1S

DEFINITION Test one's self on previously studied content by answering practice questions.

RESEARCH Beneficial in 44 of 47 studies.

BOUNDARY CONDITIONS Best when receiving corrective feedback following practice testing in free-recall or cued-recall format. Less effective when demanding only recognition (e.g. MCQ).

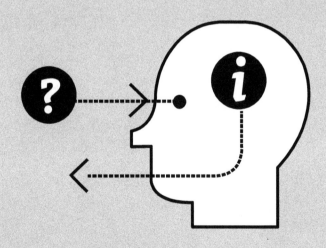

CHAPTER 5
LEARNING BY SELF-TESTING

What is learning by self-testing?

Imagine you have just changed your mobile phone number. You need to be able to know what your new number is to be able to pass it on to contacts when you need to. How might you go about achieving this? What strategies would you employ to make sure this information is quickly available to you and you are able to remember this in the longer term?

You may repeat the number a few times, you may also break it down into smaller components in order to remember parts of it before putting it all back together and maybe, if you are like me, you will write it down from memory and check if you've got it right. You may need to do this over a number of days and weeks to ensure this information remains. If you don't have to go back to this number for a while, you may need to return to it in order to check and go back through the process again to ensure it really is embedded this time.

Here you will have been employing some of the ideas around self-testing.

Self-testing in generative learning is the process in which students recall information from a learning episode, using questions or activities which require them to retrieve either specific detail or broader recollections, such as with 'brain dump' activities. So, for example, students read over a chapter of a science revision guide and then complete the questions at the end of the chapter and use the materials to check their understanding.

Unlike summarisation, which requires students to focus on just the most significant details of their learning, self-testing covers a wider range of information from the topic studied and can be used to synthesise information from a range of topics.

As with all generative learning strategies, self-testing is an approach which employs the SOI model, requiring students to select by accessing the knowledge from the learning episode appropriate to the specific question or task, organise it in a way to respond coherently and then finally integrate it into their schemata, not only by activating additional prior learning already stored in the long-term memory but also by restructuring it based on the new response they have formed.

Why use learning by self-testing?

Testing and quizzing is a frequently used strategy, especially when promoting memorisation. It is often connected to ideas of rote learning and repetition. In 1969, Allen, Mahler and Estes found that the ability to memorise information improved when people practised retrieval in comparison with restudying the materials, reinforcing its position within the classroom.[40]

However, a number of studies, perhaps most famously that by Roediger and Karpicke in 2006, indicate that self-testing and indeed low-stakes quizzing can have significant impact not only on the memory but also on the learning process itself.[41] In the Roediger and Karpicke study, students were divided into three groups and given material to study on sea otters and the sun. One group was asked to study the material four times before testing; the second group studied the materials three times and self-tested once during the learning process; and the final group studied the original material just once, and used self-testing as a method for learning three more times before taking the final test. The results showed much stronger performance from the group who had studied the material once and used retrieval as a learning strategy. This helped to provide further evidence for a phenomenon known as 'the testing effect', which had been studied since Edwina Abbot in 1909.[42]

When coupled with things such as distributed or spaced practice, testing and self-testing has the potential to further enhance the impact of learning. In 2007, Rohrer and Taylor found that students who revised material in a distributed way achieved an average of 74% on a test, as opposed to the 49% achieved by their counterparts who crammed their revision into a short period of time.[43] Therefore, encouraging self-testing over a period of time and returning to previously learned information can be a powerful tool in ensuring that knowledge is embedded into our students' long-term memories.

In a 2011 study, Argarwel and Roediger found that college students who were aware that they would be tested later in closed-book conditions were also likely to perform better as they put more effort into their initial study of the

40. Allen, G. A., Mahler, W. A. and Estes, W. K. (1969) 'Effects of recall tests on long-term retention of paired-associates', *Journal of Verbal Learning and Behavior* 8 (4) pp. 463–470.
41. Karpicke, J. D. and Roediger, H. L. (2007) 'Repeated retrieval during learning is the key to long-term retention', *Journal of Memory and Language* 57 (2) pp. 151–162.
42. Abbott, E. (1909) 'On the analysis of the factors of recall in the learning process', *Psychological Monographs: General and Applied* 11 (1) pp. 159–177.
43. Busch, B and Watson, E (2019)

material.[44,45] We all want students to think hard about their learning in order to encode it in their long-term memory and do more with the information stored within, so ensuring students are aware of these conditions could well ensure they engage with the learning materials in an active and meaningful way. Further research from Roediger et al. found myriad benefits of testing, including improved organisation of material in the minds of the students and a better awareness of gaps in knowledge and metacognitive processes, all central to the ideas of generative learning.[46]

How to use self-testing in the classroom

The most straightforward way of approaching self-testing as a generative learning strategy can simply be by asking students to write down everything they know about a topic after they have studied it. This could be combined with other strategies such as concept mapping and graphic organisers, as both will still rely on recall and transference of information from one form to another.

Short-answer quizzes at the end of chapters in revision materials, flashcards and online platforms can all be effectively deployed with retrieval.

To ensure that misconceptions and errors don't become embedded, students need to have quick access to corrective feedback, either via the teacher, their study notes or the original learning materials. Quick questions and answers on the board at the start of the lesson are a useful way to give immediate feedback to all, but it is worth ensuring everyone has corrected their errors and encouraging them to reflect on why their answers may be incorrect. This is also a good way to draw on metacognitive processes, with students identifying their own gaps in knowledge, self-correcting and reflecting on where their thinking may have taken them.

We can also utilise the testing effect by employing spaced practice strategies. Giving students a chance to retrieve information at key points, allowing time for forgetting to take place, will increase the storage and retrieval strength. Therefore, plan for opportunities for self-testing on previous topics. This can also be a good opportunity to emphasise links between topics, so in English for

---

44. Agarwal, P. K., Karpicke, J. D., Kang, S. H. K., Roediger, H. L. and McDermott, K. B. (2008) 'Examining the testing effect with open- and closed-book tests', *Applied Cognitive Psychology* 22 (7) pp. 861–876.
45. Agarwal, P. K. and Roediger, H. L. (2011) 'Expectancy of an open-book test decreases performance on a delayed closed-book test', *Memory* 19 (8) pp. 836–852.
46. Roediger, H. L., Putnam, A. L. and Smith, M. A. (2011) 'Ten benefits of testing and their applications to educational practice' in Mestre, J. P. and Ross, B. H. (eds) *The psychology of learning and motivation, vol. 55.* San Diego, CA: Academic Press, pp. 1–36.

example I may pair self-testing on key scenes in *Macbeth* with self-testing on poems which relate to this topic.

As you will see in the potential limitations of the strategy, it is also important to think carefully about the conditions of final performance. In English, I need students to have a good grasp of key facts around a text or a writer, but I also need their final performance to enable them to use that information in a fluid way. Therefore I need to create opportunities to increase fluency of retrieval and embed key information into their long-term memories but I also need to provide opportunities to retrieve that information in a more flexible way than simply answering short recap questions. Therefore using more complex questions, including drawing on that information for essay planning and writing, will enable them to retrieve knowledge when required in those conditions. This is something illustrated below in the case study which explored use of retrieval in history and geography.

Learning by self-testing across the curriculum

- In **MFL**, the learner could use self-testing to check and improve their memory of key vocabulary using flashcards.

- In **history**, the learner could use a knowledge organiser and use a read/ cover method to test their knowledge of the material.

- In **drama**, the learner could use self-testing to improve their recall, and subsequent performance, of a script.

Case study of learning by self-testing
Emma Smith (head of history) and Mark Enser (head of geography) from Heathfield Community College explored the role of the testing effect with some implications for its role in generative learning.

In 2018/19, we ran a trial for the Institute of Effective Education looking at the effectiveness of low-stakes quizzes in year 8 geography and history classes. Once a week, half of the classes sat a quick, ten-question quiz at the start of their lesson before being given the answers so that they could mark their own work. At the end of the year, all pupils in year 8 sat an assessment, and we compared how they did with their first assessment of the year. In doing this, we could examine how those pupils in the classes who completed the quizzes compared to those whose classes did not.

What we found was that, whilst everyone benefited to some extent from the quizzes, the effect was significantly greater in the geography classes than in the history classes. When we looked at the potential reasons for this, we noticed that the geography questions were often a little more complex than the history ones and needed the pupils to draw on a wider body of knowledge to answer them. So whilst in history they may have been asked to recall a particular date or name, in geography they were asked why processes took place. In hindsight, it seems possible that the geography questions were accidentally more generative in nature, requiring pupils to go through that process of selection, organisation and integration.

This has helped to shape how we use self-testing as a college, with advice to staff to think carefully about how they approach question selection in their retrieval quizzes and give thought to whether the questions require pupils to think hard about the material to be learnt.

Potential limitations of self-testing

Learners need to have good quality materials and explanations to draw on in the initial learning episode, otherwise retrieval could embed misconceptions and errors. Multiple-choice questions should be approached with caution too, as the 'lure responses' (the incorrect ones) can lead to false knowledge if not quickly corrected.

It is also necessary for learners to have the prior knowledge to draw on, so opportunities need to happen after a significant learning episode or sequence.

We need to ensure that learners are motivated to use the self-testing strategy without using the learning materials. Otherwise they will be tempted to simply copy as opposed to retrieve. Encouraging students to write down their responses is also a way to ensure they don't cut corners or assume they know the answer as they know *something* about the answer.

Corrective feedback needs to be readily available for after the retrieval, either returning to the learning materials or having access to answers, for example with flashcards or online resources, to avoid errors and misconceptions becoming embedded in the long-term memory.

The testing conditions will impact on the performance conditions, as seen in the example for English above. If you want students to be able to recall facts then test them on these only and the performance will be better than if they had not practised retrieval. However, if you want them to have greater transference and flexibility with the information, then they need to practise retrieving in this way. If we want students to transfer their learning into problem-solving situations, practising short retrieval questions will not support this well, and vice versa.

Try it out

Answer the following questions about testing as a generative learning strategy without referring to the book or your notes.

---

1. What do we call the process where we test the same concept over a period of time?

2. Who researched 'the testing effect'?

3. Give one example of a limitation that learning through self-testing could have?

4. In the case study, how many quiz questions were used at the start of the lesson?

Now return to your notes/the chapter and check your answers. Which elements were you able to retrieve? What gaps did you have? What would you need to restudy?

Further reading

Bahrick, H. P. and Hall, L. K (2005) 'The importance of retrieval failures to long-term retention: a metacognitive explanation of the spacing effect', *Journal of Memory and Language* 52 (4) pp. 566–577.

Kirschner, P. and Weinstein, Y. (2017) 'Memory and recall' in Hendrick, C. and Macpherson, R. (eds) *What does this look like in the classroom?* Woodbridge: John Catt Educational. pp. 122–142.

DEFINITION Explain the content of a lesson to oneself by elaborating on the material covered.

RESEARCH Beneficial in 44 of 54 studies.

BOUNDARY CONDITIONS Best when studying diagrams and conceptual materials, for novices and with focused prompts.

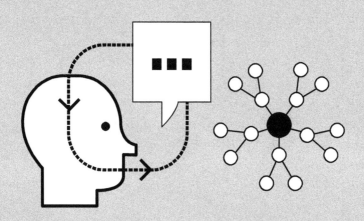

CHAPTER 6
LEARNING BY SELF-EXPLAINING

What is learning by self-explaining?

If you were asked to teach a topic you had never taught before, perhaps something you had never studied before, you would probably spend some time reading about it. As you read it, you might start explaining it back to yourself. This could involve thinking 'OK, so this must mean that...' or 'I wonder if this links to...'. This kind of thought process is the generative strategy of self-explaining and is something that many of us find ourselves doing without even being aware of it.

The activity of learning by self-explaining involves learners reading a text or diagram and then explaining to themselves what they have read. For example, a learner might read an account of the Cumbrian floods and then ask themselves 'Why was there a flood?' Alternatively, they may study a diagram of a circuit board and ask 'What would happen if I made an adjustment here?' In both cases, the learner is relating what they have just read to what they already know (the causes of floods and the operation of circuit boards in these instances).

Self-explaining can also be used as a metacognitive approach in which the learner explains why they have chosen a particular process or strategy to use. For example, after completing a maths problem, they may be prompted to ask 'Why did I complete it in this way?'

Why use learning by self-explaining?

The aim of this strategy is to ensure the learner engages with the instructional material they have been given. Through self-explaining they are having to:

- **Select** the relevant information from the material to explain by thinking about the key points and the question they have been asked or are asking themselves.

- **Organise** this information into a coherent form that allows them to answer a question or make a point.

- **Integrate** the new information into their existing schema by drawing on their prior knowledge to make sense of it.

If this is to be a *generative activity*, then this technique should go beyond simple comprehension of the text (although this might be a first step) towards the learner needing to transcend what has been put in front of them. They are elucidating greater understanding through synthesising the material with what they already know. For this reason, some prior knowledge is important; they need something to engage the new information *with*.

The aim is also to help develop more independent learners who can use the strategy of self-explaining to interrogate something new without direct input from a teacher. For this reason, it may also be a useful revision strategy. In *Strengthening the Student Toolbox*, John Dunlosky identifies it as a technique that shows promise in part because of its simplicity.[47] He points out that 'even young students should have little trouble using elaborative interrogation, because it simply involves encouraging them to ask the question "why" when they are studying'.

How to use learning by self-explaining in the classroom

To some extent, much of what we do in the classroom is already promoting self-explaining. When pupils are given an input of new information (be this from a textbook, article, diagram, map, graph, explanation or other source) they may be asked some questions about their basic comprehension, but they will also be expected to go further in generating a greater understanding of the material based on their prior knowledge. Indeed, it is very difficult to imagine a lesson where an element of self-explanation is entirely lacking.

For example:

- In art, a class might study the techniques of a painter and be asked to think about why these techniques were chosen or to contrast them to another artist they have studied.

- In geography, a pupil may be given data on the rise in CO_2 emissions and be asked why they think this has occurred.

- In history, the teacher may explain the lead up to the First World War whilst asking questions to the class about their predictions for what happened next.

However, self-explanation should go further than this and begin to ask the learner how they arrived at the answer they reached. This links to the work of Barak Rosenshine and his 'Principles of Instruction'. His third principle states that teachers should 'ask a large number of questions and check the responses of all

---

47. Dunlosky, J. (2013) p. 18

students'.[48] He says that the most effective teachers ask more questions – and more questions about the process of answering them – than less successful teachers.

To help achieve this end of pupils being able to interrogate their own explanation, we might want to teach them how to use the question stems from what is known as Socratic questioning. To do this, the learner answers a question about the material they have encountered but are then prompted to consider their answer further. This might involve them applying the following steps:

- Classify their thinking – 'What do you already know about this topic?'

- Probe assumptions – 'What additional evidence would lead to you reaching a different answer to this question?'

- Demand evidence – 'What evidence have you got for the conclusion that you have reached?'

- Alternative viewpoints – 'Who would disagree with the conclusion you have reached?'

- Explore implications – 'What are the implications for your conclusion? What would need to happen or change?'

- Question the question – 'Why do you think this was an important question to ask?'

Although self-explanation may be a normal part of everyday teaching, the work of Fiorella and Mayer tends to approach the technique slightly differently, often removing the teacher from the process and seeing it as a means for the learner to work without instruction, at least after the technique itself is taught. In fact, one application they return to throughout their book on generational activities is in remote learning. For example, on self-explanation, they say, 'Self-explaining may be particularly effective when learning from diagrams and worked examples. Further, more focused self-explanation prompting may be most useful within computer-based learning environments such as educational games and simulations' (p. 146).

When self-explaining is used away from instruction, the learner is either taught the technique and then left to apply it as they see fit or given further specific prompts prepared in advance for the material they are studying. In some of the studies discussed by Fiorella and Mayer, they found it advantageous to give the learner a menu of options for explanation to select from rather than an open

48. Rosenshine, B. (2012) p. 14

choice.[49] This might help to mitigate against the learner reaching very wrong conclusions from self-explanation in an environment where there is no one available to immediately offer a correction.

Learning by self-explaining across the curriculum

- In **maths**, before embarking on a set of questions, the learner might explain the process to themselves.

- In **science**, before completing a practical, the learner might explain the process they will be carrying out. This should enable them to then concentrate on what is to be learnt rather than the mechanism of carrying out the work.

- In **religious education**, the learner might explain to themselves the origin of the views of a particular faith on an issue being studied.

Case study of learning by self-explaining

Ceridwen Eccles has been teaching across all year groups within the primary sector for the last 15 years. She is currently teaching year 5 and enjoys applying knowledge of teaching early years and KS1 into the lessons she delivers with older children. In this case study, she explains the important role that is played by self-explaining in her classroom.

Having taught across all key stages within the primary sector, I can honestly say the one commonality I have found to unite all year groups is the fundamental concept that the greatest resource you have within the classroom is the children themselves. The ability of (even incredibly young) children to look at their own work and generate independent inquiry questions from the work produced is powerful. The tool of 'self-explaining' is one I use within the classroom, and it does just that, utilising the power of the learner to move them forwards in the depth and quality of their understanding of the subject taught.

This can be across a variety of subject areas. It might be during a maths lesson, where a child has used one method and sees that a peer has used a different method and then questions why they have adopted that approach. The ability to articulate why they have selected a certain methodology over

---

49. Atkinson, R. K., Renkl, A. and Merrill, M. M. (2003) 'Transitioning from studying examples to solving problems: effects of self-explanation prompts and fading worked-out steps', *Journal of Educational Psychology* 95 (4) pp. 774–783.

another not only strengthens their understanding but also allows them to explore a variety of strategies, which ultimately serves to make them recall and highlight a bank of knowledge that will help them in the future. I often tell the children that the knowledge I am giving them is like the strings of a harp. They cannot play them all at once, but if they have them all, they have the ability to play any tune asked of them. Self-explaining allows them to make that independent decision. And rationalise it. The dialogue generated serves to cement that learning, ensuring it is not forgotten.

I have found self-explaining within reading sessions to be particularly useful as it is intrinsically woven into the fabric of every lesson. My children are taken through the steps of vocabulary exploration and features of effect, so when we come to read a passage, they immediately start to generate questions about why an author is deliberately choosing a certain word, or why certain writing features have been adopted. We recently looked at the wonderful text Nevermoor by Jessica Townsend. We had done significant work during our 'taught' literacy sessions on features of tension writing. We then read a chapter together. I asked the children to focus on the words and techniques the author was using to scare them and wanted them to apply what we had explored – through direct teaching – independently, within the passage. The conversations were incredible. They were deep-thinking why the author had used specific words. One word that stood out was 'odious'. We had looked at that word in pre-taught vocabulary sessions and cemented the learning through daily retrieval practice. I then saw the children questioning why that word was more powerful than just 'horrible' or 'despicable'. They talked about the sensory approach and how an odious character evoked an unpleasant person through the meaning of the word and also how the link to disgusting smells served to make other connections. Kids are great aren't they! I feel the technique of self-explaining during reading sessions allows the children to have a deeper understanding of the text and therefore a deeper connection to the words on the page. This ultimately generates a greater love for and pleasure from reading. This also has an impact on the quality of writing produced, as they have explored why an author crafts paragraphs the way they do, and I see the children replicate techniques in their own writing.

Potential limitations of learning by self-explaining

There are a few potential pitfalls of self-explaining that we need to be aware of. Firstly we need to consider, once again, the time it takes to fully train the learner in how to use this technique themselves. Not only is there a time cost in teaching the technique, but carrying out self-explanation can itself take more time than other forms of learning. Fiorella and Mayer warn that 'it is important to consider the extent to which self-explaining, which can be time-consuming, offers unique learning benefits beyond other uses of learning time' (p. 141).

There are also some apparent contradictions within the literature on self-explanation, with Fiorella and Mayer suggesting it is most appropriate for those with lower prior knowledge of the topic but Dunlosky warning that high prior knowledge is needed to ensure that generation of understanding is possible and that this technique may therefore not be suitable for very young children. This could mean that there is a fine line to be walked between those learners who do not have enough prior knowledge to make use of the strategy and those whose knowledge is so high that it is unnecessary.

Try it out

You have now read a lot about six of the different generative learning strategies. Explain to yourself what you have learnt about the ways students use similar processes in these strategies.

Further reading

Dunlosky, J. (2013) 'Strengthening the student toolbox', *American Educator* 37 (3) pp. 12–21. Retrieved from www.bit.ly/2YpLDeC

Smith, M. and Firth, J. (2018) 'Independent learning' in *Psychology in the classroom*. Abingdon: Routledge.

DEFINITION Teach others about previously studied material.

RESEARCH Beneficial in 17 of 19 studies.

BOUNDARY CONDITIONS Best when students study the material knowing they will later be teaching it and so reflect on their own understanding, as well as answering peers' deep questions.

CHAPTER 7
LEARNING BY TEACHING

What is learning by teaching?

At the end of this chapter, you will be asked to teach someone else about this strategy.

As you read, think carefully about the key elements you will need to pass on and how you will explain them as clearly as possible. Most importantly in order to achieve this, you will need to check that you have fully understood the material as you will be tested on it!

Now obviously it is not within our power as authors to actually make you do this, but simply considering the notion of teaching others about this topic will have started your engagement with teaching as a generative learning strategy.

This strategy, as one might expect, is where students explain important concepts from their own learning to others. For example, students might read a text about poverty in Victorian England and then go on to teach the key ideas from that text to a partner or the class. This is a wide-ranging strategy with which many will be familiar, having perhaps used discussion, peer instruction and cooperative learning as strategies in their own settings or for their own learning.

Unlike other generative learning processes such as self-testing, there is a much lower empirical evidence base related to teaching with only 19 studies which were able to identify teaching as the key variable. In studies such as those on peer tutoring by Roscoe and Chi,[50] it has proven hard to identify exactly where the greatest impact is coming from in a process which incorporates a number of different aspects. In other words, is the impact on the learning related to the process of teaching, the process of being taught or additional factors such as instruction or guidance from the actual teacher? This is especially an issue where reciprocal teaching is used. Many studies indicate benefits from this approach, but it is not clear which element is having the greatest impact on embedding the learning and improving student performance.

---

50. Roscoe, R. D. and Chi, M. T. H. (2007) 'Understanding tutor learning: knowledge-building and knowledge-telling in peer tutors' explanations and questions', *Review of Educational Research* 77 (4) pp. 534–574.

This is why Fiorella and Mayer have focused their attention only on research which aims to isolate the teaching element from strategies such as those mentioned above.

Why use learning by teaching?

Teaching requires students in the first instance to think hard about the concepts which they are studying. In the most successful studies, students who knew they were studying to teach were more motivated in their studies of the materials and outperformed their peers who studied using different methods.

Bargh and Schul's research[51] in 1980 found that there were three distinct phases of teaching, linked to the SOI processes:

- Firstly, the preparation stage, in which students would select and begin to organise their understanding of the materials, thinking hard at this initial stage in order to make appropriate selections as they study.

- Secondly, the act of explaining encourages students to actively engage in the materials, again selecting, reorganising and drawing on prior knowledge in order to make the ideas as clear as possible.

- Finally, when interactions take place between tutor and tutee such as through deep questioning, metacognitive processes are employed as the teacher reflects on their own understanding of the material and restructures it as necessary (p. 155). In order to enhance the possible benefits presented in this phase, employing Socratic questioning techniques (see chapter 6 for more details regarding this approach) could ensure the interactions are of the highest quality.

In their own studies, Fiorella and Mayer found that students who were required to teach the materials they studied significantly outperformed others who were asked to either only study the materials or prepare to teach them without actually teaching.[52]

Those who taught materials in a follow-up study also outperformed those who had been given extra study time as well as those who studied and were given a follow-up practice test before the final assessment.

Some research has also focused on isolating the impact of the peer interaction within this strategy, using a computer-based platform to give feedback on the

---

51. Bargh, J. A. and Schul, Y. (1980) 'On the cognitive benefits of teaching', Journal of Educational Psychology 72 (5) pp. 593–604.
52. Fiorella, L. and Mayer, R. E. (2013) 'The relative benefits of learning by teaching and teaching expectancy', *Contemporary Educational Psychology* 38 (4) pp. 281–288.

quality of explanation and opportunities to reflect on what they had understood in their teaching. This indicated that those students who used the Betty's Brain computer program, where there was a teachable agent, outperformed those who did not participate with teaching as a learning strategy. In one study by Holmes,[53] it was concluded that students' learning was deeper 'when they interacted with Betty's Brain compared to when they explained without interacting with the agent' (p. 161).

How to use learning by teaching in the classroom

One application of this could be in the English classroom when studying the poetry clusters for GCSE. After some pre-teaching to address potential misconceptions, during which there is modelling of effective explanation, students are given high quality materials to support their study of the text, with the understanding that their role would be to teach another student, or students, about their poem.

Once they have studied the poem and the materials, students are given prompts to craft questions to ask each other, including questions which would encourage them to make links to their prior learning, either from that topic or other topics they had studied, for example *Macbeth*.

During the preparation stage, students are also given access to teacher guidance to again ensure that errors were not becoming embedded and students could be redirected if necessary.

Equally, teaching as a learning strategy can be incorporated in more time-limited activities in any subject area by telling learners that they will have to explain concepts from a text, lecture or video to their partner once they have studied it, giving some time to reflect before teaching so they can engage in the selecting and organising processes, before continuing to organise and integrate the information. In its most simple form, this could be through using 'think, pair, share' activities, where students reflect on their own understanding, discuss with a partner and then finally discuss with a wider group, including teaching elements of their understanding of the topic to others.

Fiorella and Mayer also point to a number of studies which seem to indicate that well designed peer tutoring programmes can have significant impacts for both tutor and tutee, for example in studies by Cloward in 1967, Morgan and Toy in 1970 and Galbraith and Winterbottom in 2011 (p. 154). This can include vertical programmes where older students tutor younger students as well as

---

53. Holmes, J. (2007) 'Designing agents to support learning by explaining', *Computers & Education* 48 (4) pp. 523–547.

those in their own age range. Again, not all of the benefits may come from the action of teaching; but if we are considering numeracy or literacy programmes which do not require specialist input, this could be an effective way to harness the benefits for all.

Learning by teaching across the curriculum

- In **drama**, each learner might study a different character before returning to the group to explain what they have learnt and answer probing questions about them.

- In **maths**, a learner might strengthen their knowledge of a technique by explaining it to others by coming to the board and demonstrating it.

- In **art**, the learner might improve their own ability in a technique by having to demonstrate it to others.

Case study of learning by teaching

Freya Odell is a teacher of English at St George's British International School in Rome. In this case study, she explains how she uses a 'jigsaw' method to give structure to how pupils may teach each other newly learnt material.

The IB learner profile asks for pupils to be reflective thinkers and learners who are knowledgeable and able to communicate that knowledge clearly and concisely. As a result, it is important that opportunities are built into the curriculum to allow pupils to be more independent in their thinking and that their confidence is developed in articulating or elaborating that thinking to their peers.

One way in which this is done at KS3 is through an increased use of the jigsaw method, which Hattie argues has an effect size of 1.20.[54] This could be used when approaching a poem, for example. Pupils would be organised into groups, with each group being given a different aspect of the poem to explore: language, structure, viewpoint, etc. In groups, pupils would work together to study the material with the focus in mind. They would pull out key textual details and discuss their interpretations before summarising and organising their learning. The teacher would then reorganise the pupils into new groups made up of pupils who had been exploring different aspects of the poem. Each person in turn would be given the opportunity

---

54. Hattie, J. (2014)

to present their learning and then take questions from people within their group. The benefits of this method are many:

Working in the initial group

- Pupils are given a space to independently respond to a text, bringing their unique insights and ideas first.

- Pupils are able to share ideas and interpretations in a safe space with their peers. This not only strengthens and increases the interpretation but also gives confidence to the ideas being articulated.

- Knowing that they will need to present their learning helps them to assimilate key information and organise it in a way that is of clear benefit to others, especially if you were to add in a timed element. The use of collective efficacy ensures pupils make serious and thoughtful contributions.

Working in a jigsawed group

- Pupils feel expert in their focus area as the ideas they are presenting come from a shared group understanding.

- Through discussion, pupils can begin to make links between the provided areas of focus, which enhances pupils' interpretations and enriches their understanding of the text.

- Pupils ask questions of each other and try to establish the answers by themselves. This leads to stronger discussion points and a range of potential interpretations being offered.

At the end of the activity, the class comes together to reflect upon their learning. The teacher drives a wider discussion, pulling on pupils' own interpretations and learned knowledge and addressing misconceptions, should these arise. However, using the jigsaw activity within the classroom is about developing the pupils' voice and confidence in understanding and interpreting key texts and supporting each other through the process rather than always being reliant upon their teacher.

Potential limitations of learning by teaching

One of the most significant issues to be aware of with this approach is the potential to embed false learning in both those adopting the role of the teacher and those being taught. Good quality study materials are required to help avoid this, alongside regular learning checks.

Equally, not all students will be able to construct effective explanations of some complex topics and they need to have a good understanding in order to do so. The students who also simply restate learning without reflecting, selecting and organising will not perform better than those using other approaches, so scaffolds to support these elements should be used in order for teaching to have the desired effect. It may be that this strategy is better placed later in the learning sequence after other strategies have been employed.

The questions and follow-up interactions can again have the potential to misdirect and create misconceptions. Also, questions which do not really probe understanding are unlikely to prompt the desired metacognitive processes.

There is also some evidence which suggests the stress and anxiety created by the possibility of having to teach and present publicly serves to 'moderate the potential benefits' (p. 181) of using teaching as a generative learning strategy. This is something to consider carefully when proposing this approach for your students, allowing for extra study time and support for those who may find this kind of interaction difficult.

Try it out

Find a colleague to explain your learning from this chapter.

Think carefully about those points from the start of the chapter: what is the key information they need to know and how will you explain it clearly?

Encourage them to ask questions to probe what you mean, even if they might understand the ideas.

Spend time reflecting on your own understanding of this strategy and restudy or look at some of the further reading to improve your understanding further.

Further reading

Jarrett, C. (2018) 'Learning by teaching others is extremely effective – a new study tested a key reason why', *BPS Research Digest* [Blog], 4 May. Retrieved from www.bit.ly/34kykyP

Pedley-Smith, S. (2018) 'The protege effect – learning by teaching', *Pedleysmiths Blog* [Blog], 29 September. Retrieved from www.bit.ly/2QdNhdy

DEFINITION   Engage in task-relevant movements during learning.

RESEARCH   Beneficial in 36 of 49 studies.

BOUNDARY CONDITIONS   Best when students already have relatively high knowledge base, as well as receiving guidance and practice. Mainly for younger children.

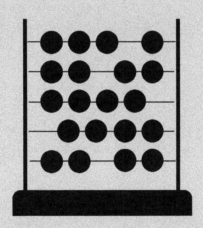

CHAPTER 8
LEARNING BY ENACTING

What is learning by enacting?

Picture the scene. You are in your car and looking for a particular street. You are lost, but luckily there is someone coming who can offer you directions. A lot of confusing directions. What do your hands start doing? If you are anything like me, they begin gesturing left and right along with the directions being given. These little automated gestures might actually help us to remember.

This technique of enacting involves the learner manipulating objects or making gestures that are linked to the thing to be learnt. For example, a group of pupils might move to enact a scene in a novel or use models to act it out. Enacting can also be used in maths where there is a physical representation of the problem being solved, such as using counters in a sum. A further example of enacting is the use of gestures to represent something to be learnt, such as hitting your hands together to represent the erosional force of attrition.

Why use learning by enacting?

One thing that enacting does is to make the abstract more concrete in the mind of the learner. It might be difficult for a young learner to picture the interaction of people in a story, but moving the characters around in the form of models might allow them to understand the events more clearly. Piaget terms the stage of pupils at around the ages of 2–7 'pre-operational'. One of the features of this stage is that children tend to see things only from their own perceptions. As Daniel Muijs and David Reynolds explain, 'Children at this stage are also very egocentric. They tend to see the world and the experience of others from their own standpoint.'[55] It is conceivable that enactment will help younger children understand a story or process from a different standpoint as they are asked to assume the mantle of that standpoint (see also the case study from Tim Taylor in chapter 4).

As with the other strategies, enacting fits into the SOI model. Information from what is to be learnt is selected by the learner. They then organise this information as they consider how best to enact it and then ultimately integrate it into their schema by making links to prior knowledge and experience through the enactment.

---

55. Muijs, D. & Reynolds, D. (2018) *Effective teaching: evidence and practice*. London: Sage, p. 24.

Enacting has also been placed within cognitive load theory (CLT): John Sweller and Fred Paas suggest that the use of gestures might help to offset some of the cognitive load of the task.[56] They explain that humans have evolved to learn some things incredibly easily. We pick up spoken language and movement without needing direct instruction in how to do this; we can learn it simply by observing others. This form of learning is termed 'biologically primary information'.[57] Other things (termed 'biologically secondary information') cannot simply be picked up; they need someone to introduce us to them. This would include things like reading and arithmetic.

Sweller and Pass suggest that those ways of learning biologically primary information, such as observing others and trying movements out, could be used to support the learning of biologically secondary information. They point to studies that show how observing human action can make replication easier[58] and how learners using gestures can lead to the lowering of the cognitive load of a task.[59] They posit that this could be because verbal information is being supported by the auditory-visual sketchpad and so is being processed by a different part of the brain.

It is worth pointing out at this stage that Fiorella and Mayer find that the evidence base for the use of enacting is somewhat weaker than their other strategies, with 36 of 49 studies in their literature review reporting a positive impact of their interventions and with a somewhat smaller median effect size than their other strategies. Keep in mind that their discussion of the strategy points out the following:

> In short, the focus of this chapter is on whether students learn academic content more effectively by manipulating physical objects themselves (or engaging in other task-relevant movements such as gestures) *compared to students who are presented with the same material but do not engage in movements.* (p. 170, our emphasis)

56. Paas, F. and Sweller, J. (2012) 'An evolutionary upgrade of cognitive load theory: using the human motor system and collaboration to support the learning of complex cognitive tasks', *Educational Psychology Review* 24 (1) pp. 27–45.

57. Geary, D. C. (2008) 'An evolutionarily informed education science', Educational Psychologist 43 (4) pp. 179–195

58. Wong, A. et al. (2009) 'Instructional animations can be superior to statics when learning human motor skills', *Computers in Human Behavior* 25 (2) pp. 339–347.

59. Broaders, S. C. et al. (2007) 'Making children gesture reveals implicit knowledge and leads to learning', *Journal of Experimental Psychology*: General 136 (4) pp. 539–550.

In other words, they are contrasting the impact of enacting with no other strategy beyond giving the information. It is not contrasted with doing something else instead. With these caveats in mind, we will explore how you might use enacting in the classroom.

How to use learning by enacting in the classroom

The principles of learning by enacting as set out by Fiorella and Mayer only really apply to younger learners who struggle with moving from the concrete to the abstract. The methods used are therefore likely to be those commonly found within the primary classroom, such as using blocks to help with counting, addition and subtraction or to show fractions and proportion. As ever when using a concrete analogy for an abstract idea, we have to be careful that the object doesn't lead to distractions or misconceptions. For example, the colours of the blocks used might either distract the learner or take on a significance in the mind of the learner that the teacher had not intended.

This technique can also be used where the learner enacts the scene from a story they are learning, either in person or through the use of models, to better commit the actions of the story to memory. This may aid comprehension of the story they are reading and therefore allow for greater understanding. They will, however, need instruction in how best to enact the material and help to see the links between what they are doing and the material to be learnt. The more abstract the material, the harder this will be to achieve.

Ideas could also be enacted in the classroom through the use of concrete models. For example, some people use cake in a geography classroom to represent the rock of a cliff and give pupils forks to represent the waves. They then enact the eating away of the rock by the waves. The difficulty with this is that a fork is a poor analogy for a wave (it behaves in a very different way) and the cake is a poor analogy for the rock (it doesn't collapse as rock does). It shows that we have to be very careful with enactment so that we don't introduce misconceptions through the use of poorly chosen analogies.

Gesture could also be used to help make the abstract more concrete. For example, if a class were learning about different erosional forces, they might bang their fists together to remember attrition or rub their hands past each other for abrasion. This would hopefully help them to distinguish between two easily confused terms.

Learning by enacting across the curriculum

- In **music**, the learner might begin by practising the movements they will need with an instrument before beginning to perform.

- In **MFL**, the learner could use a gesture when repeating key phrases or vocabulary.

- In **maths**, the learner might use physical representations of the numbers they are manipulating, e.g. blocks or beads.

Case study of learning by enacting

Tarjinder Gill is an experienced primary school teacher, having taught across both key stage 1 and 2 in disadvantaged schools in the Midlands, London and Norfolk. Her current focus is the primary English curriculum. Here she discusses how the use of gestures supports learning in her classroom.

I have used story maps to support retelling narratives in English lessons, but more recently branched out to use them to illustrate processes too (such as Ancient Egyptian embalming). The maps consist of simple drawings or icons and key vocabulary which I create for the whole class.

While this supported pupils during the initial lesson, I noticed significant variation in the ability of pupils to use the maps to recall material in subsequent lessons. I introduced the use of gestures primarily to support the recall of key vocabulary they would have had less exposure to (e.g. embalming, canopic jars). Gestures were kept simple to aid recall. At first the gestures were decided in advance and taught to pupils, but as they became familiar with the technique, pupils were able to suggest appropriate gestures.

When retelling led to a piece of writing, I would model retelling the story in chunks. Pupils would copy the gestures while saying the sentences (paraphrasing was allowed, but I would stop and correct if I could hear grammatical errors). This was repeated until pupils were secure. I would then no longer retell the story but just model the gestures with pupils recalling the story.

Pupils then took turns orally retelling the story to their partners. The pupil who was listening was still expected to join in with the gestures. Pupils were asked to retell themselves the story and check with the story map.

I found the use of gestures enhanced pupils' recall of key vocabulary and their knowledge of the sequence of the story or process. Also, the more confident pupils were when using gestures, the less they relied on the story map when retelling or writing.

Potential limitations of learning by enacting

As discussed, there are a number of potential pitfalls of attempting to place learning by enacting into the classroom. Firstly, we need to remember that the work on this largely applies to younger children who struggle with the idea of moving past concrete ideas. We should also keep in mind that of all the generative learning strategies discussed in this book, this one has the weakest evidence base.

If we are to use learning by enacting then we need to make sure that the enacting doesn't become a distraction from the thing to be learnt or create misconceptions. In the example given above of using cake in a geography lesson, the learner may be thinking about eating the cake rather than the process of erosion or they may pick up misconceptions about the way a wave attacks the cliff, seeing it as having a digging action like a fork.

There is also a danger that the actions taken during enacting create primarily episodic memories rather than semantic ones. These episodic memories are closely tied to the event that created them ('I remember acting out a scene from *Romeo and Juliet* with puppets!') but they are hard to transfer to new contexts. On the other hand, semantic memories ('I know a major theme in *Romeo and Juliet* is conflict relating to masculinity') are harder to place to a particular event but are easier to relate to other learning ('These issues of conflict and masculinity are also explored in *Lord of the Flies*'). For a further explanation of this, see Clare Sealy's work, given in further reading.

Try it out

Pick out some of the key ideas from this chapter. What gestures could accompany each one? For example, can you think of two gestures to show the difference between episodic and semantic memories?

Further reading

Sealy, C. (2019) 'Memorable experiences are the best way to help children remember things' in Barton, C. (ed.) *The researchED guide to education myths.* Woodbridge: John Catt Educational, pp. 29–39.

Stull, A.T. et al. (2018) 'Learning by enacting: the role of embodiment in chemistry education', *Learning and Instruction* 55 (1) pp. 80–92.

CONCLUSION
WHAT HAVE WE LEARNT ABOUT PUTTING
GENERATIVE LEARNING INTO ACTION?

It seems clear that generative learning has a great deal to offer teachers and our pupils. The research presented by Fiorella and Mayer shows that each strategy, when deployed effectively, has a positive effect on both recall of information and comprehension. By teaching the specific strategies to pupils, we can ensure that they develop the self-regulation to select appropriate strategies themselves and so, over time, become more independent learners, and we will leave them ready for the demands of further education or a life outside of education. By making learning easier and more within pupil agency, we should also see an improvement in motivation. They will know how to be successful.

It has also become apparent to us that generative learning fits well alongside theories of effective instruction. All these strategies require that any new information is presented to pupils in such a way that they can select from it and organise it. This means that this presentation of new information needs to be crystal clear and deploy the kind of strategies of instruction given by Rosenshine, with opportunities for retrieval, modelling, practice after small steps and regular reviews. As mentioned in the introduction, we can see generative learning as the flip-side of a coin, with Rosenshine on the other. It should not be seen as a replacement for effective instruction but provide guidance to what pupils do *after* effective instruction.

Perhaps this is one of the pitfalls that we should be aware of when introducing generative learning either in our classrooms or in our schools: the possibility that people may attempt to remove the instruction and rely instead on pupils generating learning without it. Another potential issue is that all these strategies require pupils to be trained in their use and, potentially, how they would be used differently in each subject. They then need to be used consistently and frequently if they are to have an impact. They cannot be introduced and then left.

As well as considering strategies that are appropriate for different subjects, we have to consider the stage at which they are appropriate. Enactment is likely to be of more use with younger children, whereas mapping is something we are likely to find more beneficial with those who are older. In part, this is because of their stage in development and how well they can handle abstract information; but it also depends on the amount of prior knowledge they have on a topic. Without a deep well of prior knowledge, the integration stage of the SOI model becomes weaker and more likely to lead to the development of misconceptions. As with so much else, generative learning will most benefit those pupils who are already knowledgeable.

Adopting generative learning across a school

Just like any new initiative in schools, there will be implications in terms of training. As already mentioned throughout the book, there are real time considerations with generative learning: time required to train students to use the strategies effectively and refine their use – and time to train teachers to do the same. Consistent approaches – even if that is consistency within a subject or classroom as opposed to the whole school – will always be the best way to yield the highest impact from these approaches and many others. Therefore, training needs careful planning to ensure that staff are sharing a common language and common processes around these strategies. Students will need to be instructed in how to use the strategy, be exposed to models and examples and be guided in their practice, especially if the approach is new to them.

It will therefore be essential to consider if the time investment will be significantly balanced by the impact of these strategies for your learners. What issue with your learners do you want to address by implementing generative learning in your classroom and schools? We need to consider the question, will it be worth it in our context? If the answer is yes, then it will be important to plan which of the strategies will be developed (I would consider which may have the biggest impact for your students initially and introduce others later). You need to consider how you will share your rationale and the research with your staff and consider how it will fit with existing developments taking place in your school.

Generative learning dovetails neatly with effective instruction strategies, such as Rosenshine's principles as mentioned previously. It also closely aligns with an understanding of cognitive load and schema theory. This means there are opportunities to explore strategies such as summarising alongside small steps, working memory and cognitive load. Equally, exploring self-testing and retrieval practice is effective, considering the implications of activating prior knowledge and building schemata.

In order for staff to make the best use of the strategies, they will need to be shown why the strategies will be effective and how they work, with plenty of models and examples. They then need opportunities to explore how they will work within their own subject disciplines and classrooms and plan for how they will instruct students in their use. Just as with our students, teachers will then need time to practise and refine how they teach and use the strategy, including time to reflect and review, and they will need to be supported with these processes through things such as coaching conversations.

These are all elements of good practice in relation to professional learning as outlined by David Weston and Bridget Clay in *Unleashing Great Teaching* [60] and in research by David Kolb concerning the experiential learning cycle.[61] However, it will be important to consider the time cost of implementing these strategies and what, if anything, you can afford to lose from your current list of pedagogical approaches in order to do so.

Further implications for generative learning

Fiorella and Mayer's work relates to how pupils can deploy generative strategies to the learning of new information as presented in this book. However, there are implications of their work that go beyond this purpose.

Perhaps the most obvious implication is that these strategies can be used not just to generate learning from new information but also to revise that which they have already encountered. It is notable that Dunlosky's research on effective revision has been cited in a number of our strategies and there is a great deal of crossover here. Pupils who have learnt to use self-testing and concept mapping to learn newly available information can use the same strategies to revise. In this case, they are still deploying the SOI model but are selecting information from within their long-term memories and calling it back into their working memories to be organised. At this stage, they might be able to integrate it with things they have learnt since studying the topic originally.

There are also implications for remote learning. A great deal of Mayer's research over the years has been on the use of computer-aided teaching in various forms and a reading of *Learning as a Generative Activity* reveals numerous occasions where the strategies in the book are applied via computer software in a way that attempts to remove the need for direct instruction from a teacher in the room. Pupils may be provided with information to read on the screen, or a video to watch, and then asked to deploy one of the generative strategies they have been taught. This may be an important implication where this form of remote

---

60. Clay, B. and Weston, D. (2018) *Unleashing great teaching: the secrets to the most effective teacher development*. Abingdon: Routledge.
61. Kolb, D. (1984) *Experiential learning: experience as the source of learning and development*. Upper Saddle River, NJ: Prentice Hall.

learning is a necessity (such as during the COVID-19 pandemic of 2020), but we are wary of seeing this as anything more than an act of necessity. Although it is possible for generative learning to be used to replace the teacher, it feels unlikely that it can replace the kinds of live interactions that occur in the classroom and lead to endless responses and adaptations from the teacher and the pupil in the moment.

A final implication of Fiorella and Mayer's work that we feel needs addressing here relates to the curriculum. Generative learning strategies are based on the SOI model and integration with prior knowledge is key. For these strategies to be successful, it is critically important that the curriculum is well sequenced so that there are explicit links made to what pupils have already learnt and they are made in a way that allows pupils to make the connections to what they are now learning. This implication goes far beyond the scope of this book and is likely to need a highly subject-specific approach that reflects the underlying structure of each discipline, but any teacher, or school, wishing to deploy generative learning will need to begin with a review of their curriculum.

REFERENCES

Abbott, E. (1909) 'On the analysis of the factors of recall in the learning process', *Psychological Monographs: General and Applied* 11 (1) pp. 159–177.

Agarwal, P. K. and Roediger, H. L. (2011) 'Expectancy of an open-book test decreases performance on a delayed closed-book test', *Memory* 19 (8) pp. 836–852.

Agarwal, P. K., Karpicke, J. D., Kang, S. H. K., Roediger, H. L. and McDermott, K. B. (2008) 'Examining the testing effect with open- and closed-book tests', *Applied Cognitive Psychology* 22 (7) pp. 861–876.

Allen, G. A., Mahler, W. A. and Estes, W. K. (1969) 'Effects of recall tests on long-term retention of paired-associates', *Journal of Verbal Learning and Behavior* 8 (4) pp. 463–470.

An, S. (2003) 'Schema theory in reading', *Theory and Practice in Language Studies* 3 (1) pp. 130–134.

Atkinson, R. K., Renkl, A. and Merrill, M. M. (2003) 'Transitioning from studying examples to solving problems: effects of self-explanation prompts and fading worked-out steps', *Journal of Educational Psychology* 95 (4) pp. 774–783.

Bargh, J. A. and Schul, Y. (1980) 'On the cognitive benefits of teaching', *Journal of Educational Psychology* 72 (5) pp. 593–604.

Bartlett, F. C. (1932) *Remembering.* Cambridge: Cambridge University Press.

Blunt, J. R. and Karpicke, J. D. (2014) 'Learning with retrieval-based concept mapping', *Journal of Educational Psychology* 106 (3) pp. 849–858.

Broaders, S. C., Cook, S. W., Mitchell, Z. and Goldin-Meadow, S. (2007) 'Making children gesture reveals implicit knowledge and leads to learning', *Journal of Experimental Psychology: General* 136 (4) pp. 539–550.

Busch, B. and Watson, E. (2019) *The science of learning: 77 studies that every teacher needs to know.* Abingdon: Routledge, p. 69.

Clay, B. and Weston, D. (2018) *Unleashing great teaching: the secrets to the most effective teacher development.* Abingdon: Routledge.

Counsell, C. (2020) [Twitter post]. Retrieved from www.bit.ly/326C8AJ

Dunlosky, J. (2013) 'Strengthening the student toolbox', *American Educator* 37 (3) pp. 12–21. Retrieved from www.bit.ly/2YpLDeC, p. 9.

Dunlosky, J., Rawson, K. A., Marsh, E. J., Nathan, M. J. and Willingham, D. T. (2013) 'Improving students' learning with effective learning techniques: promising directions from cognitive and educational psychology', *Psychological Science in the Public Interest* 14 (1) pp. 4–58.

Egan, K. (1986) Teaching as *story telling*. London, ON: The Althouse Press.

Fiorella, L. and Mayer, R. E. (2013) 'The relative benefits of learning by teaching and teaching expectancy', *Contemporary Educational Psychology* 38 (4) pp. 281–288.

Fiorella, L. and Mayer, R. E. (2015) *Learning as a generative activity: eight learning strategies that promote understanding.* New York, NY: Cambridge University Press.

Fiorella, L. and Mayer, R. E. (2016) 'Eight ways to promote generative learning', *Educational Psychology Review* 28 (4) pp. 717–741.

Fox, R. (2001) 'Constructivism examined', *Oxford Review of Education* 27 (1) pp. 23–35.

Geary, D. C. (2008) 'An evolutionarily informed education science', *Educational Psychologist* 43 (4) pp. 179–195.

Giesen, C. and Peeck, J. (1984) 'Effects of imagery instruction on reading and retaining literary text', *Journal of Mental Imagery* 8 (2) pp. 79–90.

Glasersfeld, E. von (1993) 'Learning and adaptation in the theory of constructivism', *Communication and Cognition* 26 (3/4) pp. 393–402.

Hattie, J. and Yates, G. (2014) *Visible learning and the science of how we learn.* Abingdon: Routledge.

Holmes, J. (2007) 'Designing agents to support learning by explaining', *Computers & Education* 48 (4) pp. 523–547.

Karpicke, J. D. and Roediger, H. L. (2007) 'Repeated retrieval during learning is the key to long-term retention', *Journal of Memory and Language* 57 (2) pp. 151–162.

Katona, G. (1940) *Organizing and memorizing.* New York, NY: Columbia University Press.

Kirschner, P. and Hendrick, C. (2020) *How Learning happens: a seminal work in educational psychology and what it means in practice.* Abingdon: Routledge.

Kolb, D. (1984) *Experiential learning: experience as the source of learning and development.* Upper Saddle River, NJ: Prentice Hall.

Leahy, W. and Sweller, J. (2004) 'Cognitive load and the imagination effect', *Applied Cognitive Psychology* 18 (7) pp. 857–875.

Leahy, W. and Sweller, J. (2005) 'Interactions among the imagination, expertise reversal, and element interactivity effects', *Journal of Experimental Psychology: Applied* 11 (4) pp. 266–276.

Mayer, R. E. (1993) 'Illustrations that instruct' in Glaser, R. (ed.) *Advances in Instructional Psychology, vol. 4.* Hillsdale, NJ: Lawrence Erlbaum Associates, pp. 253–284.

Mayer, R. E. (2014) 'Cognitive theory of multimedia learning' in Mayer, R. E. (ed.) *The Cambridge handbook of multimedia learning.* 2nd edn. New York, NY: Cambridge University Press, pp. 43–71.

Mayer, R. E and Anderson, R. B. (1991) 'Animations need narrations: an experimental test of a dual-coding hypothesis', *Journal of Educational Psychology* 83 (4) pp. 484–490.

Muijs, D. & Reynolds, D. (2018) *Effective teaching: evidence and practice.* London: Sage.

Myatt, M. (2018) *The curriculum: gallimaufry to coherence.* Woodbridge: John Catt Educational.

Paas, F. and Sweller, J. (2012) 'An evolutionary upgrade of cognitive load theory: using the human motor system and collaboration to support the learning of complex cognitive tasks', *Educational Psychology Review* 24 (1) pp. 27–45.

Pavio, A. (1986) *Mental representations.* New York, NY: Oxford University Press.

Pellegrino, J. W. and Hilton, M. L. (2012) *Education for life and work: developing transferable knowledge and skills in the 21st century.* Washington, DC: National Academies Press.

Piaget, J. (1926) *The language and thought of the child.* London: Kegan Paul, Trench, Trübner, & Co.

Pressley, G. M. (1976) 'Mental imagery helps eight-year-olds remember what they read', *Journal of Educational Psychology* 68 (3) pp. 355–359.

Roediger, H. L., Putnam, A. L. and Smith, M. A. (2011) 'Ten benefits of testing and their applications to educational practice' in Mestre, J. P. and Ross, B. H. (eds) *The psychology of learning and motivation, vol. 55.* San Diego, CA: Academic Press, pp. 1–36.

Roscoe, R. D. and Chi, M. T. H. (2007) 'Understanding tutor learning: knowledge-building and knowledge-telling in peer tutors' explanations and questions', *Review of Educational Research* 77 (4) pp. 534–574.

Rosenshine, B. (2012) 'Principles of instruction: research-based strategies that all teachers should know', *American Educator* 36 (1) pp. 12–19, 39. Retrieved from www.bit.ly/2Kw17qg

Sealy, C. (2019) 'Memorable experiences are the best way to help children remember things' in Barton, C. (ed.) *The researchED guide to education myths.* Woodbridge: John Catt Educational, pp. 29–39.

Sweller, J. (1988) 'Cognitive load during problem solving: effects on learning', *Cognitive Science* 12 (2) pp. 257–285.

Wertheimer, M. (1959) *Productive thinking.* New York, NY: Harper & Row.

Willingham, D. T. (2009) *Why don't students like school? A cognitive scientist answers questions about how the mind works and what it means for the classroom.* San Francisco, CA: Jossey-Bass.

Wittrock, M. C. (1974) 'Learning as a generative process', *Educational Psychologist* 11 (2) pp. 87–95.

Wittrock, M. C. (1989) 'Generative processes of comprehension', *Educational Psychologist* 24 (4) pp. 345–376.

Wong, A., Marcus, N., Ayres, P., Smith, L., Cooper, G. A., Paas, F. and Sweller, J. (2009) 'Instructional animations can be superior to statics when learning human motor skills', *Computers in Human Behavior* 25 (2) pp. 339–347.

Zimmerman, B. J. and Schunk, D. H. (2011) *Handbook of self-regulation of learning and performance.* Abingdon: Routledge.

CPSIA information can be obtained
at www.ICGtesting.com
Printed in the USA
JSHW040152200920
7971JS00010B/8